The Gospel

Author's Note: Read This First

If you have not read *The Awakened Woman*, put this book down.
Not because I want to sell another copy.
But because this one isn't for the woman still trying to find herself.
This one is for the woman who already has.
This book is going to touch parts of your faith you never thought
to question.
It's going to challenge your programming.
And it's going to trigger you if you haven't done the work.
And I'm not here to trigger you—
I'm here to elevate you.
I'm not here to slander religion or the church.
I grew up in it.
And truth be told, some of the values still live within me.
But a lot of it doesn't sit right with my spirit anymore.
Because when I was at my lowest—
battling anxiety, depression, and barely surviving—
nobody taught me how to save myself.
They told me to fast.
To pray.
To serve more.
To lay hands on strangers at a bus stop and trust that healing
would come through obedience.
I did all of it.

And still wanted to die.

So I had to learn how to rebuild myself.
And I discovered that the power they told me to reach for was
already *within me*.
But they didn't call it intuition.
They didn't call it discernment.
They didn't call it self-trust.

They called it the "Holy Spirit."
And maybe you've heard that before.
Maybe someone told you God lives in you.
But did anyone ever tell you that *you* were the voice?
That your gut instinct was God?
That your inner knowing didn't need to be invited in—
it just needed to be trusted?

Here's what we call it here:
We call it *you*.
We call it your divinity.
We call it your higher self.
And if that feels foreign, this book will feel like an insult to where you come from.
You won't understand the language.
You won't hear the invitation.
You'll feel attacked when I'm trying to *call you back home*.

So ask yourself:
- Have I reclaimed my voice?
- Have I faced the truth of my past?
- Have I begun to master my emotions?
- Have I stopped outsourcing my power to people, systems, or structures that never saw me clearly?
- Have I done the work to come home to myself?

If not, go back to *The Awakened Woman*.
You need that foundation first.
Because this book?
This one goes deeper.
The Awakened Woman asks you to feel.
This one will ask you to question everything that made you numb.
That book helps find your way back to yourself.

This one will help you uncover why you ever lost yourself in the first place.
It doesn't just ask: *who are you now?*
It asks: *who were you before they stripped you?*
Before the shame.
Before the silence.
Before your grandmother's grandmother was taught to hide her power.

This isn't about becoming.
This is about remembering.
Not just your healing, but your history.
Not just your light, but your lineage.
We're not here to debate. We're here to *reclaim*.
So if you're here now, that means you're ready.

Let's return.

And as you move through these pages, stay open.
Stay curious.
Stay willing to sit with what rises.
Reflection is how you keep yourself open.
Write it down, voice it aloud, sit quietly with it, give yourself space to feel what needs to be felt.
To question what needs to be questioned.
To remember what has been waiting for you all along.

And those of you that began with *The Awakened Woman*, I encourage you to revisit it occasionally—
not just to redo the activations or rituals, but to remember the exact parts of you that had to die for you to get here.
Because sometimes life will pull you out of alignment.
But if you return to what I taught you, you'll always find your way back.

Published by House of Her Publishing
Fort Myers, Florida
ISBN: 979-8-9993810-0-2

Printed in the United States of America
First Edition

Table of Contents

Chapter 1: The Lie

If you've made it this far, then it's possible—
something about the way you were taught to find peace didn't
fully work.
Or maybe…
The cover sparked enough curiosity to make you want to read,
even if you were hesitant at first.
Maybe it was the quiet realization that something didn't sit right
about how you were told to heal.
And you don't need me to tell you that.
You lived it.
You were told to pray harder.
So you did.
You were told to fast, to tithe, to submit, to serve.
So you did.
You were told to be pure. Be quiet. Be good.
So you did.

And still, your life was falling apart.
And even if I'm not talking about you—
then is it your mother struggling? Grandmother? Best friend?

Some of you have been anxious. Depressed. Numb.
Or angry and didn't know why.
You were waiting for a breakthrough that never came.
Still attracting people who weren't good for you.
Still questioning your worth.
Still wondering why your healing hadn't arrived yet—
even after you'd done everything right.
How is it that we've prayed, fasted, covered ourselves, served,
stayed silent, and still ended up lost?

Let me take you there:

- Waking up before the sun to pray.
- Fasting until your body shakes.
- Kneeling until your knees ache.
- Staying in marriages that are quietly killing your spirit because they told you a praying woman should endure.
- Giving men more grace than you give yourself.
- Being afraid of your own sensuality because you were told it was sinful.
- Still being broken while doing everything right.

It doesn't matter if you were in the church, the mosque, the temple, or no building at all—
if you've been taught that obedience equals peace, and you still feel fractured—
this is for you.
It doesn't matter what faith you come from.
Whether it was Christianity, Islam, Catholicism, Judaism, or any other religion that asked you to bow, to serve, to give more than you had to give—
to empty yourself in the name of obedience.
This message is for you.
Because across all cultures and systems, women have been taught the same unspoken rule:

Shrink.

Examples:

- In some traditions, women are asked to stay silent in the presence of men.
- In some cultures, they're asked to cover everything— even their eyes.
- In others, they're told their period makes them unclean.

- In many, they're asked to honor parents and husbands, even when those people are abusive.

And yet—
despite all this obedience, they still feel unworthy.
Still feel disconnected.
Still feel silenced.
It doesn't matter what they called it—
purity, modesty, holiness, virtue...
it all meant the same thing: *shrink*.
And when you shrink long enough, you lose your ability to feel the truth in your own body.

Now let's circle back.
To the woman who's done all the "right things" and is still attracting the wrong men.
Still outsourcing her power.
Still hoping God will choose better for her—
but hasn't yet learned to trust herself to choose better.
You can pray for a good man all day.
But if you've never been taught to trust yourself, you'll keep entertaining devils in disguise.
You'll keep calling red flags "tests from God."
You'll keep waiting for confirmation, when what you needed was conviction.
You'll keep begging the Divine to send someone better, not realizing *you're* the one with the final say.

That's why we don't just teach prayer here.
We teach self-trust.
We teach discernment. Embodiment. Nervous system wisdom.
We don't wait on signs—
we *feel* them. In our bodies. In our bones.
This isn't just about religion.

It's about remembering that the tools we needed were always inside us.
But someone renamed them. Repackaged them.
And told us we had to earn them through obedience.
They called it the Holy Spirit. We call it intuition.
They called it surrender. We call it embodiment.
They called it submission. We call it self-protection.
Somebody's got it wrong.
And now we're finally calling it out.

The Residue

Some of you have read books meant to spark inspiration or transformation.
Self-help books. Healing books. Books on growth, faith, purpose.
Told yourself, *"Yes, this is exactly what I needed."*
And some of you are brand new.
Fresh to this kind of fire.
Still unsure if you're even allowed to feel this much truth in your body.
Still figuring out what to call this thing that's waking up inside you.
But whether this is your first taste or your final straw—
I can feel that you're still waiting for a softer permission.
Still waiting for someone else to confirm what you already know.
Still hiding under titles, roles, and routines that are killing you.
And that's why I'm pissed.
Because I've been trying to wake women up.
Because I've offered what you needed to free yourself.
Because some of you have already felt the truth in your body.
And still—
you're shrinking.

You're doing everything but trusting yourself.
Everything but owning the truth that's been screaming inside of
you for years.
And that's not because you don't know better.
It's because you're afraid to live like you finally believe it.

Let me say it again for the ones still hoping to be coddled.
This is not that book.
This book isn't here to make you feel safe in your silence.
It's here to burn through every last bit of residue.
Every trace of the lie that said you needed to be small to be holy.
That said you had to earn your worthiness through suffering.
That said your voice had to be approved before it could be heard.

So before you move to the next chapter thinking you can bring
those old habits with you—
sit down and tell the truth.

And if you can't do that, stop reading now.
Come back when you're ready to burn through the illusion.

Reflection Questions

1. What were you taught obedience would give you?
   And what did it actually cost you?
2. Where in your life are you still shrinking, even now?
3. What parts of you are still hiding behind "being good"?
4. What are you still performing for the approval of people
   who benefit from your silence?
5. Why are you still outsourcing your power after everything
   you've learned?

Journal Space

Don't write what sounds good. Write what burns.

_____

_____

_____

_____

_____

_____

_____

_____

_____

_____

_____

_____

_____

_____

_____

_____

Chapter 2: Before the Burning

Let me ask you something.
What did you feel in your body the first time you heard me say the word ritual?
Be honest.
Did something tighten?
Did you flinch a little?
Did your stomach drop or your shoulders tense—
just a little?
What did you associate it with?
Because let's talk about that.
The church doesn't usually say ritual, does it?
So what came up for you when I used that word?

And what about this one: Witchcraft.
What just happened in your body?
Did it send a chill up your spine?

Now let's go a little deeper:
Words like rootwork, conjure, bloodline, altar.
What were you taught to think of when you heard those words?
What faces flashed in your mind?
What kind of energy did your body associate with them?

See, it's not just about belief—
it's about conditioning.
Because when I say church, temple, or mosque—
you don't flinch.
When someone says the blood of Jesus Christ—
nobody gets scared.
But when we say the blood of our ancestors, suddenly it's demonic?

Why is that?

Why have we been taught to fear what is ours?

Why were we taught that power outside of us was holy…

But power within us was something to run from?

And if you don't ask these questions, if you don't check the reaction in your own body—

you'll never realize that the fear was planted there.

Fear that was never yours to begin with.

Because before they reprogrammed us, before they called our wisdom witchcraft…

Before they made us afraid of our own gifts—

they burned us.

Literally.

They drowned us.

Hung us.

Set us on fire.

They held public trials and called it justice.

They threw us into rivers for the "swimming test."

If we floated, we were witches.

If we sank, we were innocent.

They killed us either way.

They said women who bled with the moon, women who healed with herbs, women who spoke to spirit without a priest—

were a threat.

And they were right.

We were a threat.

But not to people.

To power.

To systems built on control.

To patriarchy dressed in religion.

During the European witch hunts, which spanned roughly from the 1400s to the 1700s, and in some places even later, thousands of women—
especially midwives, herbalists, seers, and healers were accused of witchcraft and brutally executed.

Many were:
- Burned at the stake publicly
- Hanged or drowned
- Tortured until they confessed to things they never did
- Targeted simply for knowing how to use herbs, for speaking their truth, for not conforming

These were not just random executions—
They were organized systems of spiritual and social control.
When Christianity spread through Europe, and later colonized lands, anyone who held onto earth-based traditions or ancestral wisdom was seen as a threat.
And here's the truth that hits the hardest:
These weren't just white women in Europe.
Black women, Indigenous women, and women across colonized continents were also labeled dangerous, wicked, or "unclean" for practicing their native spiritual traditions.
See, in Europe and colonial America, women were targeted simply for being too much.

Too intuitive. Too wise.
Too sexual. Too independent.
Too poor. Too loud.

Midwives. Herbalists. Widows.

Women who didn't attend church.
Women who lived on the edge.
Women who didn't bow.

And once the burning stopped?
They kept going.
What they couldn't kill, they rewrote.
What they couldn't erase, they demonized.
And so your grandmother's grandmother...
She stopped speaking to the moon.
She stopped putting her hands on her belly.
She stopped passing down what she knew.
Because she was scared.

And now here you are—
flinching at words that used to belong to you.
And now, we hesitate to light a candle.
We whisper about burning sage.
We're scared to say we use herbs out loud.
Because the spell is still working.
But sis...
Before the burning, before the shame, before your grandmother's
grandmother ever learned to bow her head in someone else's house
of worship—
there were women who weren't afraid.
There were women who gathered under the moon.

Who bled freely.
Who used herbs to heal.
Who danced.
Who touched the earth and knew she would answer back.

There were women who spoke to spirit directly.
Without a priest. Without a book. Without fear.
And those women?
They are your inheritance.
They didn't leave you with shame.
They left you with memory.

The ache to remember who you were before you were taught to be small.
The whisper in your belly when something doesn't feel right.
The pull toward nature.
Toward healing.
Toward rhythm.
That isn't rebellion.
That's remembrance.
And now, you get to choose:
Keep shrinking?
Or start returning?

Reflection Questions

1. What words still carry fear in your body?
2. What have you been taught to avoid, dismiss, or label evil without ever exploring it for yourself?
3. Where are you still hiding your spiritual practices to avoid judgment?
4. What "god" were you taught to fear more than you were taught to love yourself?
5. What did you stop doing, or never started, because someone told you it was wrong?
6. When was the last time your body said yes, but your religion said no?

You don't need to name everything right now.
You just need to know —
There's more.
And your body already knows the way back.

Journal Space
Don't write what sounds good. Write what burns.

_____

_____

_____

_____

_____

_____

_____

_____

_____

_____

_____

_____

_____

_____

_____

_____

_____

_____

_____

_____

Chapter 3: The Theft Was Global

It wasn't just your people.
It wasn't just your grandmother.
It wasn't just your church, your childhood, or your community.
This erasure? This rewriting?
It was *global*.
And it didn't just steal land.
It stole language, lineage, memory, and power.
Across the world, women were once the carriers of wisdom.
The herbalists.
The doulas.
The midwives.
The oracles.
The healers.
But the more powerful they were, the more threatening they
became to empire.
So colonization didn't just kill culture.
It reshaped it.
It rewrote it.
It renamed it.

Let's name what they tried to bury:

Sarah Baartman: When Curiosity Became Exploitation

Sarah Baartman was a Black woman from the Khoekhoe people of
South Africa.
She was brought to Europe in the early 1800s, put on display as a
"freak show" attraction because of her body—
her curves, her hips, her buttocks.
They didn't see her as human.

They called her the "Hottentot Venus," and paraded her body in circuses and private shows like an object.
Even after she died, they didn't stop.
Her body was dissected. Her genitals and brain were placed in jars and displayed in museums.
They dissected her then.
And they're still dissecting us now—
On operating tables, in music videos, in algorithms built on our curves but blind to our souls.
And to strip us of power, they first had to strip us of *dignity*.

Colonial India: When Womanhood Was Recast

In India, British colonizers redefined the roles of women by filtering them through a Western, Christian lens.
Practices that once centered women—
like birth rituals, communal healing, spiritual leadership—
were erased or rewritten.
Practices, like *Sati* (widow burning), were weaponized to justify colonization.
But they erased the richness and range of Indian womanhood, reducing it to either "barbaric" or "submissive."
Before colonization, many Indian women held spiritual and social authority.
After colonization, they were silenced in the name of "civilizing."

The Loss of Language: Erasing the Tongue of the Ancestors

Colonizers didn't just steal land, they stole language.
Indigenous and African dialects, rich in oral tradition, were outlawed or mocked.
Why?
Because in those words lived spells.

Because those words weren't just words.
They were tools—
Ways to protect, to name, to remember who we were before we were forced to forget.
And who held those languages?
Women.

Women passed down songs, birth stories, herbal knowledge, ancestral truths.
So silencing women meant silencing history.
When you can't name something, you can't pass it down.
When you can't speak your truth in your mother's tongue, it starts to fade.
This is how they buried our power—
not by killing it, but by renaming it.
And let's talk about that.

Hoodoo and Conjure: African American Spiritual Traditions

Hoodoo, also known as Conjure or Rootwork, is a traditional African American spiritual practice that emerged during slavery in the United States.
It blends African spirituality with Indigenous knowledge and European folk magic.
It was never a religion. It was a system of survival.
Of protection and power.
Rootworkers used herbs, roots, minerals, and prayer to heal, to shield, to call in what was needed.
It was intimate.
It was intuitive.
And it was deeply connected to the land and the ancestors.
It wasn't evil.
It was *ours*.

Vodou (commonly misnamed "Voodoo"): A Syncretic Religion of Power and Resistance

Vodou developed in Haiti as enslaved Africans blended their
traditional religions with Catholicism.
Why?
Because colonizers banned African spirituality.
And so they hid it behind Catholic saints.
But make no mistake—
the deities, called lwa, were not the saints.
They were powerful forces—
honored through dance, drums, offerings, and spirit possession.
Vodou was central in the Haitian Revolution.
It wasn't just spiritual. It was revolutionary.
It helped birth the first free Black republic in the Western
Hemisphere.
That's what they feared.

Demonization by Design

These practices weren't demonized because they were dangerous.
They were demonized because they couldn't be controlled.
Because a woman who knows how to call on her ancestors,
who trusts her body, who speaks to spirit directly—
can't be manipulated.
So they gave it another name.
They called it dark.
They called it demonic.
And we've been afraid to return to our power ever since.

But not anymore.

Let me be clear.
This chapter isn't about making you angry.

You don't need to carry rage to carry awareness.
You don't need to pick up resentment to reclaim your roots.
You're not here to fight the world—
you're here to *remember yourself.*
Some people will read stories like these and get stuck in the
trauma of it all.
But not you.
You're not here to live in grief.
You're here to move with grace through the truth.
So take what resonates.
Ask the questions.
Trace the roots.
But don't carry anger as your offering.
Carry clarity.

That's how we change the narrative—
not by staying wounded, but by walking in wisdom.
And just in case you're reading this and asking,
"Is this woman trying to make me believe in witchcraft?"
then ask yourself... why?
Why does that word still scare you?
Why have you grown so accustomed to *their* language that *yours*
now feels foreign?
It's not "witchcraft."
It's your history.
Your heritage.
Your power.

Why can the church use oil and herbs to heal, lay hands on the
sick, give offerings, light candles—
and that's seen as holy?
But when we do it—
with our herbs, our roots, our sacred tools—
Suddenly it's dark?
Make it make sense.

And I already know what the next rebuttal's going to be.

"Well, it depends on the intention behind it."
But who's setting the intention? Is it you or them?
And the women who've crossed paths with me—
The women I've held.
Sat with.
Prayed over.
The ones who've seen me use incense, sound bowls,
herbs, and oils...
Do I feel dark to you?
Do I feel unholy?
When you hear my voice...
When you read these pages...
When you witness how I love, how I teach, how I hold space—
Do you feel darkness?
Or do you feel light?

Here's the truth...
I'm a walking contradiction to everything they told you.
I broke the spell.
I left the shame.
I reclaimed my roots—
Without bowing to anything dark.
All it took was remembrance.
I remembered that the power was in me the whole damn time.
So no—
I'm not here to convert you.
I'm not here to prove anything.
I'm just offering you the mirror.
And like we did in *The Awakened Woman*—
all I'm asking is that you question the why.
Why do you believe what you believe?
Where did it come from?

Who gave it to you?
And what did they gain by keeping you afraid of your own power?
That's what this chapter is about.
Not belief.
But liberation.

And lastly…
Baby, if they can have altars then so can we.
This isn't just history.
This is *your story*.
Somewhere in your lineage, someone experienced a version of this theft.

Reflections Questions

1. What have you been taught to distrust about your own culture?
2. What have you seen labeled as "dark" that you're starting to see differently?
3. Whose approval are you still subconsciously seeking when it comes to your spiritual path?
4. What rituals or practices have quietly called to you but fear kept you from exploring them?

Journal Space

Don't write what sounds good. Write what burns.

_____

_____

_____

_____

_____

_____

_____

_____

_____

_____

_____

_____

_____

_____

_____

_____

_____

_____

_____

Chapter 4: The Gifts Were Never Lost

I used to think I had to become something.

I thought I had to learn more.

Study harder.

Get certified.

Prove I was enough.

I thought wisdom had to come from books.

From pastors.

Or elders.

That power had to come from outside me.

But then I started remembering.

not in my head—

But in my body.

In my bones.

In the way I just knew things without being taught.

That's when I realized…

What I thought I was becoming, I already was.

And what I thought I had to chase—

was passed down to me.

Because gifts don't die when our people do.

They linger. They wait.

They live in our hands.

Our habits. Our hunger for something more.

In the way we call bullshit before a lie even finishes forming.

In the silence we hold when everybody else is performing.

In the way we feel spirit before we have the words.

And when we're ready—

they rise.

We've spent enough time naming what was stolen.

Now, let's name what was passed down.

Let's talk about the women they never taught you about.

The conjure women.
The seers.
The midwives.
The medicine women.
The dreamers.
The women who were never given titles but carried the entire village on their backs.

So let me explain...
A conjure woman wasn't a witch.
She was a healer.
A rootworker.
A woman who knew how to use the plants, the earth, the fire, the prayers passed down by word of mouth.
She knew how to protect her people when nobody else could.
She didn't call on demons, she called on the ancestors.
She was creating safety in a world that refused to give it to her.

A seer is someone who sees beneath the surface.
She has visions, dreams, or sudden knowings.
She can feel what's unspoken. Sense what's hidden.
Sometimes she calls it discernment.
Sometimes it shows up as anxiety—
But it's not anxiety.
It's ancestral knowing trying to get your attention.

A midwife wasn't just there to catch babies.
She stood at the threshold of life and death.
She knew how to bring life into the world—
and how to guide souls back home.
Her wisdom wasn't taught in medical school.
It was remembered.

And the medicine woman?
She didn't write prescriptions.

She remembered what the land offered.
She knew which leaves to boil for pain.
Which roots to chew for fever.
Which rituals to perform when the energy in the house felt heavy.
She didn't get her wisdom from textbooks—
she got it from the land.
From listening. From lineage.

Now think about this:
What if the thing you've always been drawn to isn't random?

What if your calling to natural hair care is about healing through the crown because our ancestors knew the scalp was sacred?

What if your love for skincare isn't just about aesthetics, but about restoring radiance to the face of women who forgot they were divine?

What if you're drawn to the medical field because you're remembering how to tend to the body in a world that keeps ignoring it?

What if your desire to become a therapist isn't just about helping people cope, but about guiding them back to truth?

What if you're a lawyer not just because you're articulate and brilliant, but because you carry the ancestral imprint of truth-tellers and justice keepers? Because your bloodline remembers what it means to defend what is sacred.

What if you work in construction, electrical work, or plumbing— not just to build and fix, but because something in you remembers how to restore what's been broken. Because your hands are gifted. Your energy stabilizes. You're anchoring energy into places that need grounding.

What if you're in law enforcement or security, and your calling isn't about control, but protection.
What if your lineage remembers how to shield and guard the village? And this role is how that instinct still moves through you.

What if you're in the military, a truck driver, or doing heavy lifting every day, and something in you still feels spiritually responsible for the safety of others? What if your body is strong because your lineage required it, but your softness is sacred too?

What if you work in finance—
not because you love numbers, but because you're remembering that money is energy. And you're meant to learn how to circulate it with intention, not fear. Because your people were once stripped of wealth, and now you're learning to reclaim it.

What if your corporate job isn't a distraction from your purpose, but the exact place Spirit placed you to disrupt old systems with new frequency? What if the boardroom needs your fire?

Sis... the point is:
You don't have to leave your job to be spiritual.
You don't have to quit your career to be sacred.
You just have to recognize the role your soul already signed up for. Because sacred work doesn't only happen in retreats and rituals. It happens in courtrooms, classrooms, break rooms, job sites, patrol cars, and kitchens. It happens wherever you show up.

You don't need to change your title.
You just need to honor your essence.
And honor it—
wherever you are.

The Harvest *(Interlude)*

We were taught anything outside of colonized religion was evil.
Not because it was.
But because they needed you to believe it was.
They couldn't afford for you to remember who you were, so they
called your birthright wicked.
They stripped the intention, twisted the narrative, and turned
something sacred into something shameful.

And you believed it.

You believed it because harm was done in its name.
Because somebody, somewhere, used what was meant for healing
to hex, to scare, to control.
And now, you think that was the original purpose.
But that's not the truth.

It's like handing someone a machete.
Not to kill—
but to harvest.
To clear the land. To feed the village.
To protect what's sacred and till what's ready to grow.
But then they use it to harm.
So now, generations later, all you see is the blood on the blade.
You forgot about the fruit.
You forgot that it was made for life.
The machete didn't change.
The intention did.

That's what they did to our ancestral tools.
They demonized what they couldn't dominate.
They desecrated what they didn't understand.

And then they handed you back your inheritance with a warning label.
So now anytime something doesn't look like your church, your Bible, your colonized Jesus, your hallelujah—
it's evil to you.
But it was never about evil.
It was about power.
And more importantly—
what you were taught to do with it.

Let's name it:

Vodou (not "voodoo")—A religion rooted in Haiti, born from West African spirituality mixed with Catholicism during colonization. It was built to honor spirits, heal the body, and protect the soul. Not hexes. Not dolls. Not demons.

Hoodoo—Not a religion, but a practice of African American folk magic, rooted in the survival of enslaved people in the U.S. It used herbs, roots, candle work, and spoken word to shield, to bless, to call back power when everything else was stripped away.

Yorùbá & Ifá—An ancient West African cosmology centered on harmony, ancestors, and the Orishas—divine forces of nature. It's about balance, destiny, and listening to spirit.

Santería— A Cuban tradition that blends Yorùbá cosmology with Catholic saints. It was born in the shadows of colonization when enslaved Africans were forced to mask their gods behind saintly faces. Beneath the surface, it carried drumbeats, divination, offerings, and the Orishas. It was never witchcraft. It was resistance in disguise.

Palo Mayombe— A spiritual tradition from Central Africa, brought to the Caribbean by enslaved Bakongo people. It centers on working with spirits of the dead and the natural elements— earth, fire, water, metal, and wood. Practiced through sacred altars called *ngangas*, it's used for healing, protection, and spiritual justice. Misunderstood by many, Palo is not evil—it's ancestral technology rooted in survival.

Christianity—A religion based on the crucifixion and resurrection of Jesus Christ, centered on salvation, grace, and eternal life. It was carried across the world through missionaries and colonization, often replacing the spiritual systems of entire cultures. While the teachings of Jesus were rooted in love, the institution built around him was rooted in control.
It renamed gods. Erased languages. Called ancestors demons.
And trained people to fear anything that didn't sound like a Bible verse or come from a man behind a pulpit.
For many of us, it was our first introduction to God.
But we were taught to enter through fear, not freedom.

Now let's get real.
Y'all don't worry about candles until they're sitting next to some herbs and a glass of water.
You light candles on Saturday morning while you're cleaning your home, playing old R&B or gospel in the background.
You use oil every day—
on your skin, in your hair, in your skillet.
You drop it in a diffuser to shift the energy in a room.
You drink water. Bathe in water. Play in water. You *are* water.
It's never made you nervous before.
And herbs?
You season your food with them. You boil them for tea.
You grew up on peppermint, Vicks Vapor rub, and ginger root.
So tell me why it's different when intention gets involved.

Actually... I'll tell you why.
Because it's not about the candle.
It's not about the oil.
It's not about the water.
It's not about the herbs.
It's about what you've been taught to *fear*.

The moment you put those elements together in sacred practice,
your conditioning kicks in.
You don't even question why.
You just see a name—
Hoodoo, Vodou, Palo, and decide it's evil.
But it's not the name, it's the narrative.
It's not the practice, it's the perception.

This is not about converting you.
It's about correcting the record.
Because the real danger was never the practice.
It was the erasure. The silence.
The fear you inherited from the people who feared your power.
And when you finally stop confusing darkness with depth, stop
mistaking remembrance for rebellion, you'll realize—
what you've been calling evil... was your liberation all along.

I don't think you need reflection questions.
You just need to be willing to sit with this and ask, *why*.
Why, at the very least, did you not do the research yourself instead
of allowing someone to tell you what to believe.

Are you afraid your curiosity may turn you into something?
Are you still holding on to the idea that their version is the only
truth?

Chapter 5: The Womb Was Never the Enemy

I didn't always know there was such a thing as a sacred womb space.
I wasn't raised with that language.
I didn't grow up hearing that my blood was powerful.
Or that my body could remember. None of that.
But something shifted.
I had already done the work to find myself.
I had reclaimed my voice. I had faced my pain. I had begun healing.
And yet...
I found myself wondering, *what more is there?*
If I've done all this healing—
Why does it feel like I'm just now scratching the surface?
That's when I started thinking about where I came from.
Not just spiritually. But biologically. Historically.
I started getting curious.
And not about anatomy.
I was curious about what had been stripped, renamed, and hidden.

I don't even remember the exact moment I came across the idea of the womb as sacred.
But I remember how my body reacted.
Like something clicked.
Like something ancient whispered, "Yes."

I used to think my period was just a damn inconvenience.
Cramps. Bloating. Back pain. Breakouts. Cravings.
The cravings made the bloating worse. The bloating made the cramps worse.
Everything felt like too much.
And I hated it.

Not just the pain, but the way I was expected to keep going.
We aren't allowed to slow down just because we are bleeding.
We were expected to keep working.
Keep smiling. Keep showing up.
Even when we were hurting. Even when we were tired.

And so I did.

I thought that's just what being a woman meant—
carrying the weight and not complaining too much about it.
But when I finally slowed down enough to listen, something else
emerged.
I wasn't just uncomfortable because of cramps.
I was uncomfortable because I had been trained to see my cycle as
a problem.
Not a process.
Not a portal.
Not something to revere.
And that's when it hit me:
Wait a minute… what did my ancestors believe about bleeding?

I started digging.
And what I found changed everything.
They didn't just strip our land.
They stripped our rhythms.
They stripped our rest.
They stripped our reverence.
They turned what was once seen as sacred into something to be
hidden, silenced, and shamed.
But my womb hadn't forgotten.
She was still trying to tell me.
She wasn't just bleeding.
She was remembering.

And before we go further, I need to say this:
If you no longer bleed—
this chapter is still for you.
Maybe you've entered menopause.
Maybe you've had a hysterectomy.
Maybe you've never bled.
No matter your journey—
your womb is still sacred.
Womb wisdom isn't reserved for the bleeding.
It's not about a cycle, it's about a center.
It's about the seat of memory, intuition, power, and presence.
Your womb still holds.
Still speaks.
Still remembers.

So as you read about bleeding, shedding, releasing—
know that these are metaphors too.
They are sacred patterns.
And you are still a part of them.
You don't need blood to be connected.
You just need breath. Intention. Presence.

History: What Our Ancestors Knew

Before colonization and capitalism told us to push through the
pain, there were women who paused.
Women who treated this time as sacred.
Across cultures, menstruation wasn't something to hide.
It was a time of power.
A time of rest.
A time to receive.
And this rest wasn't earned.
It was expected.

- In West African traditions, like those of the Dogon people of Mali, menstruating women rested in sacred huts — Not because they were exiled, but because they were honored.

- In parts of North America, Indigenous tribes like the Ojibwe built moon lodges — spaces where women would retreat during their cycles. Elders would pass down stories. Visions were received. Menstruation was seen as a heightened spiritual state.

- In South Asia, Ayurvedic tradition taught that a woman's body was cleansing during her cycle. She wasn't expected to perform. She was encouraged to rest, eat grounding foods, and honor her rhythms.

These weren't just traditions.
They were truths.
Truths that were stripped, renamed, and shamed out of us.
Because a woman who listens to her body?
A woman who rests when the world says rush?
A woman who honors herself when the world says sacrifice?
She's dangerous.
She's powerful.
She cannot be controlled.

Years ago, I was diagnosed with endometriosis.
The pain was unbearable.
At first, I thought something was wrong with me.
But somewhere deep inside, I knew —
it wasn't just my body.
It was my inheritance.
My womb was holding on to things that weren't mine to carry.
So I started changing the way I treated her.

I adopted a plant-based diet. I detoxed. I listened.
I tracked not just my cycle, but the messages inside it.
The texture, the color, the timing of my blood.
And without even realizing it, I was remembering.
Not through books. Not through teachers.
Through my body. Through my spirit.

One night, I lit candles—
not for mood, but for something I couldn't name yet.
I started setting intentions before sex.
Whispering affirmations at the peak of climax.
I didn't realize it at the time, but I was practicing sex magic.
Not because someone taught me.
Because my body remembered.

I was doing rituals long before they ever told me what to call them.
I knew. I've always known.
Even the birth of my daughter was sacred.
I refused pain meds. I trusted my body.
I moved through every contraction, not knowing my ancestors
were beside me.
But now I see it.
There was a point where the pain got so unbearable.
I had been laboring for about 21 hours.
And I remember telling my mother, "I'm so tired... just give me
the epidural."
It took the anesthesiologist a while to come.
I lost track of time—
like I wasn't even there anymore.
My mother said it took about an hour for them to arrive.
And when they walked in, I remember them trying to force that
needle into my back.
And the contractions?
They got stronger. Closer.

I kept telling them, "My baby is coming."
But they wouldn't listen.
Looking back now…
I can see my ancestors with their hands on my shoulders saying:
"No. We got this."

And every time they tried to force that needle through, my body
answered with another surge.
Contractions like drumbeats.
Louder. Sharper. Refusing intrusion.
Something ancient in me rising up to say:
"No. We got this."

They tried to force me to be still.
To control me instead of listening.
But my body knew better. My soul knew better.
It wasn't just labor. It was rebirth.
My womb remembered.
And before the medicine could completely numb my body, my
baby was crowning.

Your womb is not a curse.
She is a portal.
She is an altar.
She is the memory keeper.
She holds grief.
She holds wisdom.
She holds the blueprint for your becoming.
And she will speak—
If you slow down long enough to listen.
I didn't just learn this through research.
I lived it.
One night, deep in the bleeding phase of my cycle, I woke up in
the middle of the night in excruciating pain.

It wasn't just discomfort—
it felt like my body was trying to purge something from my spirit.
I stumbled into the shower, too weak to stand for long.
So I sat beneath the stream of hot water, letting it pour over my
chest, my heart, my womb.
And I said these words aloud:
I wash away everything that doesn't belong to me.
I wash away anything tethering me to an old life.
I wash away anything weighing down my spirit.

I didn't feel immediate relief.
But something shifted.
I felt lighter. Unburdened.
When I laid back down, I placed my hands over my heart and
womb.
And I whispered:
I see you.
I honor you.
I trust you.

And then I surrendered to sleep.
That night, my womb spoke to me.
I dreamt that I was in a public restroom.
A woman that I recognized leaned over the stall and began fanning
me.
I looked up, confused.
And she sneered:
"You stink."
At first, I felt shamed.
Exposed.
Then I felt angry.
Because I realized she was talking about my blood.
She was shaming my blood.
I stormed out of my stall, pulled her from hers, and attacked her.
Not because of the insult. Not because of her words.

Because my womb was rising in my defense.
Because my ancestors were roaring:
Your blood is not shameful.
Your blood is not dirty.
Your release is sacred.

My interpretation of this dream is that it wasn't about violence as
it may seem—
it was about reclamation.
This was about every woman who was ever told her body was
something to hide.
This was about the ancient memory inside me saying:
Protect what is sacred.

This was the first time I ever honored my womb in this way—
and she spoke back to me so clearly.
Immediately, I knew I needed to wake up and write it down.
She doesn't just bleed.
She speaks because she remembers.
And she will protect what is sacred inside of you.

Womb Ritual

During your next menstrual cycle, I want you to come sit with me.
Maybe not physically, but spiritually. Energetically.
To release—
not just blood. But the stories your womb carries.
Even if you no longer bleed, your body still remembers.
Here's what I love to do:
First, I take a hot shower.
I love the feeling of the water running down my body.
While I'm in there, I whisper to my womb and thank her.
I tell her it's okay to release the old.

It's safe to make room for the becoming.
I tell her that I trust her.
And listen, you don't even have to say it out loud.
Just say it to yourself. Feel it.

After I step out, I like to slow down and really take my time.
I start with my skincare—
my face routine first, and then I reach for my cocoa butter.
I take my time rubbing it all over my body, moving slow, not
rushing. I do it as an act of reverence for myself.
And I'm not rushing to get dressed.
Because my body deserves to be honored, even in the small
moments.

While I'm doing this, I have my raspberry leaf tea steeping.
And now that I'm paying more attention to my womb, I notice she
craves this tea around this time every month.
It's like she knows.
Raspberry leaf tea has so many benefits —
it strengthens the uterus, supports healthy flow, and helps your
body shed fully and deeply. It's not just tea. It's medicine.

And sis...
I almost feel like we need a snack too, right?
How do you feel about yogurt-covered raisins?
I know we usually crave something sweet around this time, but
Spirit won't let me reach for anything too artificial or heavy
anymore. So yogurt-covered raisins it is for me.
But what about you?
What can *you* bring into this moment to make it even more sacred?
Now it's time to really set the mood.
I love to light a vanilla incense stick.
Maybe one formulated for grounding.
Sometimes a candle too.
And in the background, I'll have some soft lo-fi music playing.

Just enough to fill the room without taking up too much space.
Because you deserve to bring beauty into every sense—
Your touch, your sight, your taste, your hearing.
It's simple.
It's soft.
It's sacred.
Not because you're doing a ritual perfectly.
But because you're allowing yourself to slow down.
To listen.
To be with yourself.

So next time you're bleeding, come sit with me.
You're not just shedding blood.
You're shedding the old story that says you have to keep rushing
when your body is asking you to rest.
And that, all by itself, is enough.

The Body Remembers

Let's be honest—
this world wasn't built to honor your cycle.
So I'm not here to guilt you if you can't take a day off.
I know some of you have jobs.
Kids.
Commitments.
I see you.
I honor you.
But even if you can't rest during the day...
Can you rest after the sun goes down?
Can you light a candle after the house is quiet?
Can you pour a cup of tea and sit with your womb for five
minutes?

Can you put your phone down and just say:
I see you. I hear you. I'm listening now.

Sacred doesn't mean pure or perfect.
Sacred means set apart.
It means you slowed down long enough to honor something—
even if it's messy.
Even if it hurts. Even if it's you.
So if you're bleeding, aching, stretched thin…
What would it look like to offer yourself reverence?
Not a perfect ritual. Not a performance. Just a pause.
To say:
I'm not just tired. I'm sacred.
I'm not just moody. I'm powerful.
I'm not just bloated. I'm shifting.

Sacred doesn't require incense.
It requires honesty.
And that's where healing begins.

And sis…
If you no longer bleed?
You're still invited.
Because like I said earlier—
bleeding is also a metaphor.
A metaphor for release. For renewal. For making room.
Some of us are shedding trauma.
Some are grieving old versions of ourselves.
Some are breaking family patterns.
Some are birthing businesses, visions, courage, or boundaries.
And all of that? That's womb work, too.
Your womb is a portal.
This is where the midwife shows up.
Not just for babies, but for breakthroughs.

For letting go.
For pushing through.
For coming home to yourself.
Your womb doesn't need to shed to speak.
She still remembers.
She still holds.
She still guides.
So whether you're in your first cycle, your final cycle,
or no cycle at all—
this space is yours, too.

Reflection Questions

1. What have you believed about your womb that you're ready to let go of?
2. What emotions do you feel during your cycle that you usually ignore or push through?
3. What would it look like to honor your body *exactly as she is*—not just when she's performing, but when she's resting, releasing, remembering?
4. What messages has your womb tried to send you lately?
5. What is she holding that you haven't yet acknowledged?
6. If your womb is a portal, what is she asking you to birth, or bury, right now?

Journal Space

Don't write what sounds good. Write what burns.

Chapter 6: The Stirring

There are going to be moments on this journey where you feel
something before you can name it.
Where something cracks open inside you, but you don't have the
language for it yet.
And I want you to know:
That doesn't mean you're not ready.
It means you're already in it.
When I wrote *The Awakened Woman*, I included a story in Chapter
11—a ritual, with J. Howell's *Rocket* playing, a moment that felt
something rising in my body.
At the time, I didn't know what it was.
But I trusted it.
And now I know—
that was Kundalini.
That was the fire starting to rise.
That was ancestral remembrance flowing through me before I had
the words to explain it.
I'm not writing this book from theory.
I'm writing this book in the middle of my own becoming.
My life is the text.
This page is being born in real time, while I'm in the shower,
while I'm driving, while I'm making voice notes to myself just so
I don't miss the message.

That's how alive this is.

Most people journal once a day.
Me? I'm journaling all damn day.
Because Spirit don't wait for a convenient time.
She speaks when she speaks—
and I refuse to miss it.

Sometimes it's a whisper.
Sometimes it's a wave.
Sometimes it's a headache so deep I know my third eye is wide the fuck open and I need to wrap my crown in a scarf just to stay grounded.
But I don't question it anymore.
I stay open.
So what does it mean to stay open?

It means:

- You let the question hang without rushing to answer it.
- You feel the pull without forcing it into form.
- You know you don't need to read every book, memorize every chakra, or get every certification just to trust what's already moving through you.

It means you stop saying, *"I don't know enough,"* and start saying, *"I know what I feel."*
It means you stop silencing what's rising because you don't know the right words and start trusting the language of your body.
This book was born because I stayed open.
I didn't wait until I had all the definitions.
I didn't wait until I could explain every tradition, every practice, every term.
I started writing because I felt the flame—
and that was enough.
And maybe that's where you are right now.
Maybe you've felt things you couldn't name.
Maybe you've been doing rituals without even realizing they were rituals.
Maybe you've touched sacred wisdom without knowing your ancestors passed it down to you.

Don't wait for permission.
Don't wait for a title.
Don't wait for someone to explain what you're already
embodying.

If your spirit is stirring. If your body is vibrating. If your truth is
rising...
Then you are already on the path.
Let this be the confirmation.
You don't need to know all the names.
You don't need to sound "spiritual enough."
You don't need to be fluent in sacred language.
You just need to stay open.

Because when you do?
The remembrance will find you.
The words will come.
The ancestors will whisper.
And you'll realize:
You've been carrying it this whole time.

Let's Talk About the Fire

Kundalini isn't just an idea—
it's a force.
She lives at the base of your spine, coiled like a serpent.
And the moment you acknowledge her?
She stirs.
I didn't know what I was doing at first.
But my body did.
The first time I truly felt her rise was in the mirror—
while self-pleasuring.
One hand on my breast. One hand between my thighs.

Looking myself in the eyes.
Not rushing. Not chasing climax.
Just being there. With myself. For myself.

And then it happened.

The fire didn't shoot up like lightning.
It started thick, slow—
like honey warming in a jar.
A pressure curled at the base of my spine, and I could feel it
climbing—
slow and steady, like heat building in a furnace.
Thick. Sticky. Sweet.
Like something ancient had been sleeping there and was finally
waking up.
It wasn't just arousal.
It was remembrance. It was power.
It was the sensation of my soul re-inhabiting my body.
The pull moved through my root. Melted into my sacral.
Ignited my solar plexus. Expanded into my heart.
Opened my throat. And somewhere between my third eye and
crown, I realized this wasn't about climax at all.
This was a ceremony.
And that's when I felt the explosion.

And what's wild is...
I used to be afraid of snakes.
Even the thought of them would make my skin crawl.
But lately—
my body has been moving like one.
Slow. Sensual. Intentional.
Not in fear, but in power.
I didn't try to become the serpent—
I remembered that I already was.

They told us the serpent was evil.
That she lured Eve into sin.
That she sparked the downfall of humanity.
But what if that story was never about sin at all?
What if the snake she listened to is the same one I'm speaking of now?
The same one coiled at the base of your spine, waiting to be honored.
What if she didn't taste forbidden fruit—
but tasted herself?
Her knowing.
Her desire.
Her body.
Her God-given power.

What if Eve wasn't tricked, but initiated?
What if that moment wasn't the fall, but the first rise?
What if that wasn't the end of innocence, but the beginning of remembrance?
Because tasting yourself—
claiming your pleasure, your power, your presence.
That's not sin.
That's sovereignty.
So maybe the story's been wrong this whole time.
Maybe the snake wasn't the villain.
Maybe the snake was the teacher.
And maybe the garden was never lost—
just buried beneath everything they told us to be afraid of.

Kundalini didn't rise because I summoned her.
She rose because I remembered her.
Because I made space for her.
Because I finally said, *I'm ready*.
That's what opened the door.
And now I know better.

This energy, this force—
it doesn't belong to monks and gurus.
It belongs to women.
But like any sacred force, she must be honored.
To nourish her is to create safety in your body.
To slow down.
To feel what you've been afraid to feel.
To breathe into your hips.
To soften your jaw.
To stop performing and start listening.
To protect her is to stop letting just anyone near your body.
To stop giving your energy to people who drain you.
To stop ignoring your intuition when she says no more.

Because the fire within you is sacred.
And sacred things aren't rushed.
They're not picked apart.
They're not explained to people who never deserved access in the
first place.
So when she rises in you—
care for her.
Make space for her.
Don't try to control her.
Just honor her.
That's how you stay open without leaking.
That's how you stay soft without shrinking.
That's how you rise without burning out.

But before we go any further—
I need to speak to the woman who isn't sure she's ready.
Because for some of us, the mirror is more terrifying than the altar.
Maybe you don't feel safe touching yourself right now.
Maybe the idea of looking at your own body with love feels far
away.

Maybe this fire I've been writing about feels more like a flicker.
Or a wound.
If it feels foreign, maybe it's because no one ever taught you your
body was yours.
If it feels frightening, maybe it's because someone taught you
through shame, silence, or violation—
That your body was dangerous.
That your pleasure was sinful.
That your desire made you dirty.
That your power was something to be managed, not embraced.
And if that's your truth—
I see you.
You are not behind.
You are not broken.
You're just remembering.

Maybe you flinched when I spoke about self-pleasuring.
Maybe your throat tightened when I said "Kundalini."
Maybe a part of you whispered, *this chapter isn't for me*.

But I want to tell you—
it is.
Your body doesn't have to respond like mine.
Your healing doesn't have to look like anyone else's.
Your sacred doesn't have to be sexual.
It just has to be *true*.
If all you can do right now is breathe, cry, or be still—
that is holy.
You don't have to do it all.
You just have to stay open.
Because that's where the fire begins.
That's where remembrance finds you.
And that's exactly where we'll meet.

If you're ready, step through.
But don't bring your shame with you.

Activation

Get naked.
Not just in body, in truth.
Look at yourself in the mirror.
Not with makeup.
Not with lashes.
Not with soft music playing in the background.

Just you.
Just your skin.
Just your breath.
Just your eyes.

And ask yourself:
- When's the last time I touched myself without guilt?
- When's the last time I looked at my own body and didn't criticize something?
- Do I even know what I like? Or have I just been trying to perform what looks good?

And deeper still:
- Do I feel safe in my body?
- Does my womb feel safe with me?
- When I close my eyes and breathe into my lower belly... does it feel open? Or locked?

Breathe.

Now ask:

- Who am I still letting access my body, even when my spirit says no?
- Who am I still trying to impress?
- What part of me is still afraid of being fully seen?

And if your body starts trembling—
let it.
If your eyes start watering, don't wipe them yet.
If your womb starts throbbing, pay attention.
Because this isn't just a mirror.
This is a portal.

And let me tell you something—
the first time I leaned in close and stared into my own eyes
while my body moved like a serpent, I flinched.
The energy shot up my spine so fast it scared me.
Not because it was dark, but because it was *real*.
Because I *felt* something awaken.
And I turned away.

We've been conditioned to fear what we see in the mirror.
To cover it at night. To avoid holding our own gaze for too long.
Why?
Because the mirror doesn't just reflect your face, it reflects your frequency.
It shows you what's stirring in your soul.
And if you've spent your life hiding, suppressing, performing—
it'll shake you.
But baby, don't look away this time.
Because once you walk through it?
You don't un-know what you know.
You don't un-feel what you feel.
You don't un-see the parts of you that are waking up again.

This isn't about an orgasm.

This is about remembrance.

When you feel ready, begin to touch yourself like you're holding sacred ground.

Speak to yourself like you're talking to God.

Move like the flame is already lit inside you.

Because it is.

And baby... you're the altar now.

Reflection Questions

1. What did your body feel during the Activation? (Tingling, warmth, tightness, resistance, openness)
2. Did any part of you want to look away? What might that part be protecting?
3. What part of your body feels the most alive right now? Can you breathe into it with gratitude?
4. If your womb, chest, or throat could speak right now... what would she say?
5. What are you remembering that you didn't realize you had forgotten?

You don't need to have the perfect words.

You don't need to write it beautifully.

You just need to be honest.

Because presence *is* the practice.

And safety begins in truth.

Journal Space

Don't write what sounds good. Write what burns.

_____

_____

_____

_____

_____

_____

_____

_____

_____

_____

_____

_____

_____

_____

_____

_____

_____

_____

The Reckoning *(Interlude)*

Be still.
Because if you just moved through that activation and felt
something stir—
and you're still trying to call it darkness?
Check again.
If you skipped the activation, if you turned the page instead of
turning toward yourself—
then ask why you're still running from your own reflection.
And although you couldn't face that mirror, there's still one
waiting for you on this page.

I'm the mirror.

So I'm asking you now…
Why do you keep trying to find demons in anything that doesn't
wear a robe?
Hell, y'all do it to the modern church too.
Because the pastor wears jeans now.
Because the message sounds different than what you heard at your
grandma's church.
It's demonized.
And why?

You've been conditioned to fear your own reflection.
To fear your own fire. To fear your own voice.
Because they knew—
if you ever remembered, you wouldn't need them anymore.
The women who've met me know who the fuck I am.
They know what they feel when they're in my presence.
If something inside you is still trying to call this evil?
You're not afraid of me.
You're afraid of what I woke up in you.

But what are you really afraid of?
That the mirror might show you a version of yourself you buried to survive?
That your gifts, the ones you hid to make others comfortable—
Might still be in there waiting?
That your rage might actually be righteous?
That your power isn't demonic, it's divine?
You think this discomfort is about me?
It's about the you that's waking up.
You can burn this book.
You can call it dangerous.
But don't say I didn't offer you a mirror.

And before we move on...
I'm going to ask: Do I need to invite you back to your reflection?
I know some of you didn't skim or look away.
You stood there.
You saw yourself.
You heard her.
But I felt the need to pause for the ones still running.
The ones still whispering, *"I'm not ready."*
Go back.
You can't read your way into remembrance.
You have to face yourself.
So I'll pause.
I'll wait.
Because the woman on the other side of that mirror?
She's still waiting on you to come home.

Chapter 7: The Indictment

In *The Awakened Woman*, I discussed the purpose of masculinity
and the ways it shows up in relationships.
How the wounded masculine tends to control, avoids
responsibility, and destroys trust through inconsistency and
manipulation, while the embodied masculine protects, leads with
integrity, and creates safety.

But I want to talk more about what I've witnessed.
I've spent most of my life navigating the aftermath of men who
haven't done their work.
Men who love us.
Men who live with us.
Men who say we're "their world"—
but don't know a single thing about the history they inherited, or
the damage they're still doing.

This is the indictment.

Because it's not just about abuse.
It's not just about the ones who scream or hit or abandon.
It's about the quiet ones.
The "good guys."
The ones who say "I love you" with their mouths while draining
our life force with their entitlement.
They don't even know they're doing it.
They don't realize that the roles they expect us to play.
Cook, clean, raise the babies, smile while doing it—
are rooted in a history of dehumanization.
They don't know that the reason we're so fucking tired is because
we've been taught to serve and soothe, even when we're starving
inside.
They don't know the bloodline.

They don't know the breakdown.
They don't know the cost of being a woman who loves a man who never learned how to hold space.
And when they slide into our DMs looking for a heart react or a thank you, when they expect access just for giving us a compliment, they don't realize they're reenacting the same entitled ritual that's lived in their lineage for centuries.

They don't need to grab us by the throat to be dangerous.
They do it with silence.
They do it with avoidance.
They do it by loving our softness and never earning our safety.
I don't come soft anymore.
Because I'm tired of men expecting softness from women they keep cutting.
I don't come humble anymore.
Because I've humbled myself into exhaustion.

I come sharp.
I come clear.
I come with a scalpel in one hand and a mirror in the other.
Because they may not be predators in public—
but some of them are predators of the spirit.
And we're bleeding out in their presence while they swear they mean no harm.

This is the indictment.

For every man who says he loves women but hasn't learned a single thing about what breaks us. What bends us. What burns us.

This isn't hate.
This is history.
And I'm the one reading the charges.

They say "not all men," but all women carry the imprint of what men have forgotten.

We carry the daughters who were married off too young, the mothers who birthed babies and buried their dreams in the same breath, the women who bled out in silence—

physically, emotionally, and spiritually because there was no room for their fullness in a world built around fragile masculinity.

This isn't just our story.

This is the story of women who were never allowed to speak.

And now that I'm speaking, I will not bite my tongue to protect the comfort of the uninitiated.

You want to know why I come so sharp?

Because I remember what it felt like in my bones before I had the language.

Because I've watched the women in my family, multiple women—

Crumble under the pressure of relationships and marriages that never served them, never poured into them, and only demanded their silence in return.

I've seen women shrink.

I've watched them whisper their power in kitchens and closets because the living room was his domain.

We were taught to be soft so we wouldn't be hurt.

We were taught to perform so we wouldn't be abandoned.

We were taught to serve so we wouldn't be seen as selfish.

And the worst part?

So many women are still staying.

Still carrying the illusion that this is just what love looks like.

That this is normal.

That this is what we're supposed to endure.

I'll tell you this...

Ain't nobody telling you to leave that man.

But if you're going to stay, you better stop lowering the bar to meet him.

You better stop allowing "he's just human" to be the reason you keep accepting emotional scraps.
Because yes—
he's human.
But so are you.
And if your humanity isn't allowed to rage, to rest, to receive, why are you protecting his?
Why are we normalizing men staying emotionally stunted while we stretch ourselves into spiritual contortionists just to keep the peace?
Why are we calling it loyalty when it's really just fear?

If you're going to stay, fine.
But hold him higher.
Because some of y'all are in relationships with men who can't even say why they believe what they believe—
men who inherited broken systems but never questioned them.
Can't answer a single fucking question about why they move the way they do.
And the moment you ask "why," they say you're doing too much.
When really? They just don't want to look in the mirror.

But I want to know why—
Why do you have a hard time expressing your emotions?
What kind of leader do you want to be?
Where do you see yourself in five years?
Is there something you've been dreaming of that you've been too afraid to start?
What's stopping you from becoming the man you say you want to be?
What are you still carrying from your past that you haven't named out loud yet?
How do you want to love better? Show up better? Heal deeper?

And they don't hear questions—
they hear confrontation.
So instead of answering, they say:

"You're doing too much."
"Does everything have to be that deep?"
"I'm not one of your clients."

Insinuating I'm acting like a therapist.

And I'm supposed to play along?
Pretend that's enough?
No.
Because if you can't even answer my questions—
How can I trust you to lead anything?

And here's what I'm saying to you.
Stop letting "I'm just human" be the excuse for spiritual
immaturity.
Stop letting "well, I'm trying" be the reason you carry the entire
relationship on your back.
Stop making room for men who refuse to do the work.
Because that's not grace.
That's self-abandonment.

Revelations 4:44 *(Interlude)*

If you're a woman who decided to flip to the middle of this
book...
If you skipped the beginning, rushed past the foundation,
didn't take the time to slow down and actually *feel* what I've been
saying—
And now you're here, reading this, and it's making you squirm?

Good.

You thought this was just a cute book with a spiritual aesthetic.
A little incense and intuition.
A little sacred softness.
Now look at you—
sweating.

You were warned.
You were told to start at the beginning.
To take your time.
To move slowly.
But you didn't listen—
like y'all rarely do.
Y'all listen to everybody but your damn self.

And maybe that's not what's making you uncomfortable.
Maybe it's not even that I called *you* out.
Maybe what really made your chest tighten...
Is that I called out the *man*.
Your pastor.
Your husband.
Your brother.
Your son.
You saw their faces when I read the indictment.

And now you're unsettled, but not because I lied.
You're unsettled because I named what you've been avoiding.
You've been calling it love.
But it's really been silence.
You've been calling it loyalty.
But it's really been fear.
And I don't think you're angry at me.
I think you're grieving the truth.
The grief of realizing that someone you trusted, someone you needed—
might've been part of your harm. Or someone else's.
Instead of letting it break you open, you turned it into rage.
But that rage?
That flinch?
That sting?
It's sacred.
It means the spell is breaking.
So feel it.
And then come back to the table.
Because the work you tried to skip is the very work that would've saved you.

Let me tell you something else.

Before I ever got to this moment—
before I found the language to name what I'm naming now, I went through phases.
I wanted to be a nurse.
I thought I'd work at the sheriff's office long term.
I opened a business.
I began building a nonprofit.
I studied psychology.
I even considered becoming an OBGYN.
I was just trying to find my way.
Trying to figure out why I was here.

And there was a time when I was convinced, I wanted to be a surgeon.
I never fully understood the pull.
Until one day, mid-conversation, Spirit yanked the veil off.
I was telling someone how I used to obsess over surgery videos, how I could watch people being cut open for hours.
And I never wanted to look away.
Something about it captivated me.
And right in the middle of that conversation, it hit me.
I wasn't called to cut open bodies.
I was called to cut open truth.
I wasn't meant to stitch skin.
I was meant to split illusions.
To open spirit.
To expose what was never supposed to stay hidden.
To perform holy surgery with words instead of scalpels.
And now, I'm peeling you the fuck back.
Layer by layer.
Lie by lie.
Comfort by comfort.
And baby—
this isn't just a scalpel.
This is chemo.
This is radiation.
Just in case I missed something hiding beneath the surface.
Because I'm not just here to make you feel better.
I'm here to pull out the cancer.

I've been getting cracked open for years.
About five or six years ago, something shifted.
I began studying the Holy Bible.
But not like most people.
I thought I was doing it to defend it.
I suddenly wanted to go to Sunday school every week, and not with people my age.

I sat with the elders.
I asked the deeper questions.
And in that, Spirit started pulling me back to myself.
I became obsessed with studying.
I had sticky notes all through my study Bible, so I could flip to specific verses.
And what was I bookmarking?
Scripture about false prophets.
I couldn't explain it then.
But now I understand.
I wasn't just studying to grow.
I was studying to protect myself.
I was in a space that didn't feel safe, and I needed to be able to see the ones who weren't called.
I was armoring up.
Not because I was questioning God—
but because I was beginning to see that not everyone behind the microphone had been appointed by Spirit.

But let's be clear.
It wasn't just the bad doctrine.
Not just the "sow this seed, get this blessing" lies.
Not just the "come to the altar and be healed" promises that left me still waking up wanting to die.
No, something did happen.
There was a young man in the church.
Someone that had touched me inappropriately.
And I told the pastor.
And yet...
They still ordained him to minister to the children.
And I wasn't the only one he had done this to.
I also found out he was also involved with the pastor's daughter.
And I had to sit with that.
With the silence.

With the fact that the people who preached protection were protecting predators.
You want to know when the unraveling started?

Right there.

Because why are y'all preaching righteousness while putting people like that in position?
Why do people have to armor up just to sit in your sanctuary?
Why don't people feel safe with y'all?
You can call this "church hurt" if you want.
But the truth is—
this isn't hurt.
This is harm.
And I'm not here to protect the places that didn't protect me.

So if you're reading this and feeling defensive, uncomfortable, tight in your chest?
That's your spirit speaking.
Listen to it.
This part of the book isn't for performance.
It's not here to be palatable.
It's here to confront what has been rotting beneath the robes.
I trained for this without even knowing I was in training.
And now that I'm intentional?
I'm calling it all out.
The rituals.
The rules.
The bullshit.
The reasoning that don't make sense.
The silence that kept women like me bound for years.
And if it breaks you open?

Good.
You needed it.

And let me be even clearer:
I am the scalpel. I am the chemo. I am the mirror.
I am the one that was called—
and they didn't even know it.
I've been getting nailed to the cross for *years* just to get to this
moment.
I've held back. I've played nice.

But not anymore.

You call it blasphemy?
I call it resurrection.
You think it's pride to say I'm made in God's image?
Well why would God give me this mind, this wisdom, this
discernment—
just to shame me for using it?

I didn't read a book to know what I know.
I didn't make a deal with the devil.
I wasn't praying to some shadow god in secret.
This came from within.
This came from Source.
This came from my fucking bloodline.

I walk into rooms and see broken women everywhere.
I don't say it with judgment—
I say it with ache.
Because I've lived it. I recognize it.
And I was built to cut through it.
I watch the baddest, prettiest, most powerful women show up
online looking like they've got it all...
and I still see the fracture behind the filter.
I still see the ache they don't post.
Because Spirit made me a seer.
And a healer.

And a motherfucking resurrection.

So if you made it this far into this book?
You're not just reading anymore.
You're laying on my table.
And I'm about to go in.
You can fight it.
You can flinch.
You can curse me.
But you won't leave untouched.

This is Revelations 4:44.
The end of pretending.
And the beginning of everything real.

Chapter 8: The Exorcism

What if you're wrong about everything you've been practicing
over the years?
I'm serious.
What if?
Why does that question make you so uncomfortable?
What would change about your life if you found out none of this
was true?
Would you stop breathing?
Would you lose everything good you've built?
If this way of living, this faith, was really the way you were
designed to live, then why would anything change?

Think about it…
Some of y'all have thriving businesses.
Some of y'all are raising beautiful, healthy kids.
You're fed.
You're clothed.
Your bills are paid.
You're traveling.
You're falling in love.
You're glowing.
You're living.

So tell me…
If nothing about your goodness would change without this
religion, why are you still giving it the credit for your life?
Why are you still outsourcing your power to something outside of
yourself?
You're not thriving because you bowed to fear.
You're thriving because your spirit knew how to survive despite it.

When I left the church, I was told I would spiral.

That I would fall deeper into sin.
That I would lose myself or my "salvation."
But that's not what happened.
I didn't spiral.
I didn't suddenly want to sleep around.
I didn't suddenly want to drink more.
I didn't suddenly want to club more.
Or do whatever people do to numb their shit.
I got clear. I got free.
My taste changed. Completely.
I changed on a cellular level.
I felt the shift in my body.
And that's how I knew—
I woke up.

Tell me what happens in your body when you have the audacity to
question the "what if?"
Does your spirit feel lighter?
Or does fear clamp down on your chest?
Does the very thought, *damn, what if this is all a lie*—
make you flinch?

If so, why?

Are you ready to admit that all of this was built on fear?
That maybe...
Just maybe...
You're afraid the illusion might start crumbling—
just because of your curiosity?
And if your whole religion can be threatened by a single question,
doesn't that sound like a weak foundation for something you built
your entire life on?
I'm going to let you sit with that.
And still —
I wont pretend to know more than you do.

I don't know if the God they taught me about would flood the earth and drown every man, woman, child, and animal— and still call Himself merciful, like He did in Genesis 6.

I don't know if the God who claimed to bless generations would turn around and curse entire bloodlines for the sins of their fathers, like it says in Exodus 34:7.

I don't know if a God who is supposed to be unchanging would regret His own creation—not just once, but multiple times, like it's written in Genesis 6:6 and 1 Samuel 15:11.

I don't know if the Spirit that lives inside of me— the same Spirit Jesus said would guide us into all truth in John 16:13, needs to be filtered through the mouth of another man before I can trust it.

I don't know if a God of healing would let faithful women die on cracked knees—begging for deliverance that never came, like we were promised in James 5:15.

I don't know if a God who is love would stand by while the word "homosexual" was deliberately inserted into Scripture in 1946 to rewrite the meaning of sin— twisting 1 Corinthians 6:9 into something it was never meant to say.

I don't know if the God who called Himself just would punish 70,000 people just because one man disobeyed, the way He did with David and the Israelites in 2 Samuel 24:15.

I don't know if faith the size of a mustard seed— the same faith Jesus talked about in Matthew 17:20, was supposed to leave whole generations drowning in poverty and despair inside of stained-glass prisons.

I don't know if salvation, if it was ever really a free gift— should come with fine print, tithe envelopes, and terms and conditions like the churches built around Galatians 2:16 and 2 Corinthians 9:7.

I don't know if the Kingdom of Heaven— the one Jesus said was already within us in Luke 17:21— was ever supposed to be something we spent our whole lives chasing outside ourselves.

Even when the verses stop making sense, my body still tells the truth:
I know what my spirit feels when the room goes quiet.
I know what my chest does when it's not fighting to stay small.
I know what my blood remembers when I stop pretending I'm lost.
And it's not fear. It's freedom.
It's not shame. It's sovereignty.
It's not damnation. It's deliverance.
And if they call it rebellion?

Good.

Because I didn't come here to carry their guilt.
I came here to carry my crown.
And if the fear of hell is the only reason you refuse to question the "what if"—
Then maybe you need to ask yourself:
Why would you want to believe in something that depends on your fear to be true?

Chapter 9: The Interrogation

I went to my dad to have a conversation because I needed to know why the fuck he taught me what he taught me.
Not in an argumentative way. Not to disrespect him.
But because if I'm going to start unraveling what I was taught, I deserve to know why it was ever handed to me in the first place.
That's the least we can do—
Go back and ask the ones who gave us the script:
Where did this come from? And why did you believe it before giving it to me?

This chapter isn't about dishonoring your parents.
It's about refusing to stay silent in the face of inherited confusion.
Somewhere along the way, we were conditioned to believe that we needed someone else to decode God for us.
That unless a pastor or a book or a verse confirmed it, it couldn't be trusted.
That the voice inside us—
our discernment, our intuition, our inner knowing—
Was too dangerous, too unreliable, too close to sin.
But that's a lie.
You don't need someone else to translate Spirit.
God already speaks your language.
I went into that conversation with my dad looking for clarity, and what I found was confirmation:
That we've been *performing belief* instead of embodying truth.
And I was no longer willing to pretend.

I started the conversation by asking him a memory that had resurfaced—
something I couldn't shake...

"Why did they wear those white cloths on their heads during the
Christmas plays at church?"

I remembered it clearly—
people wearing white shawls, draped and silent during the
reenactments of the birth of Jesus.
It had always seemed symbolic, but I never thought to question it.
Until Spirit brought it back to me.
He told me it was called a prayer shawl, and explained what he
had learned:
That it's something worn during prayer.
That the blue tassels at the ends represent healing.
That the knots carry meaning tied to scripture.
He gave me the explanation—
what it's called, what it represents, how it was used in biblical
times.

Then I asked him the real questions:
"Okay, but what does it do for you?"
"If it represents healing, has it ever healed anything in you?"

That was the moment he couldn't answer.
He paused.
Circled back to the tassels. Back to what he'd learned.
But he couldn't say what it stirred in *him*.
He didn't say it grounded him.
 Or centered him. Or brought him closer to God.
He couldn't tell me how it moved him—
Because it didn't.
And that's not a failure of faith.
That's a reflection of what we've all inherited:
A belief system built on repetition, not relationship.

We were taught to perform rituals, but never to ask if they were actually doing anything to us—
for us.
We know what the shawl *means*.
But not what it *does*.
And if it really carries the power, we say it does, then the question should be easy:
"What has it healed in me?"
And if the answer is "nothing," then why are we still putting it on?

Then he brought up my baptism.
Like it was supposed to prove something.
Like the fact that I got baptized meant I was aligned, obedient, devoted.
But I had to tell him the truth.
I got baptized because I was told to.
That's it.
Not because I had a personal revelation.
Not because Spirit moved through me in a way I couldn't deny.
Not because I felt ready to surrender to a higher calling.
But because someone in a position of spiritual authority said, *"It's time."*
And like most of us, I listened.
Because we're trained to follow orders, not to ask questions.

"I got baptized under the assumption that my life would be different afterward. But it wasn't. Nothing changed."

That's the part nobody talks about.
They tell us baptism is this holy initiation.
They say once you go under, you come up new.
But no one prepares you for the moment you realize you feel exactly the same.

Still lost. Still confused.

Still trying to figure out what it means to be "saved."

He responded by explaining that in biblical times, people had to take a three-week class before being baptized.

They had to fast, study, and prepare.

And maybe that was supposed to make it more meaningful.

But all it showed me was how much of our spiritual lives have been built on rituals we're expected to perform, not truths we're encouraged to feel.

So I asked him:

"What if you didn't have the Bible? What would you rely on then?"

That's when everything shifted.

Because without realizing it, I had just yanked the foundation out from underneath everything he'd been taught to stand on.

And again—

this isn't about *him*.

This is about all of us.

We've been taught that the Bible is the only channel.

That if it's not written, it's not real.

But I wasn't asking him to stop believing.

I was asking:

What happens to your faith when the manual disappears?

Can you still feel God in your bones?

Can you still discern the truth in a room full of silence?

Can you still trust your own knowing without a verse to back it up?

Because to me, that's where faith begins.

Not in certainty, but in surrender.

Not in memorization, but in relationship.

And with all this talk about trusting your voice and inner
knowing—
the conversation pivoted, again...
And he didn't answer with clarity.
He answered with fear.
He told me the devil talks to people too.
He said the devil visits people in their dreams.
And I had to pause.
Because whether he realized it or not, that's exactly how the
church trained him—
to fear his own inner voice.
To doubt his own knowing.
To believe that if a message didn't align with a Bible verse, it had
to come from the devil.
That's what they do when you get too close to trusting yourself.
They bring up hell.
They bring up deception.
They bring up confusion.
Not because they've seen it—
But because they were warned about it, and the warning became
scripture.

But here's the thing...
If I'm made in the image of God, then why would God confuse
me?
Why would the voice that speaks to my spirit sound like a threat?
Why would the dreams that bring me peace and clarity be treated
like spiritual sabotage?
His response said everything about the system that raised him:
Don't trust yourself. Don't trust your thoughts. Don't trust your
dreams.
And above all—
Don't question what you were taught.

But I'm questioning anyway.
Because I don't believe God would gift me discernment and then shame me for using it.

After that moment, I realized—
this was never just a conversation with my father.
It was a confrontation with everything that tried to train me out of trusting myself.
Because that's the danger of blind belief.
You stop listening. You stop asking. You stop feeling.
And that's exactly why I wrote *The Gospel*.
Not to tell people what to believe.
But to invite them to *feel*.
To return to their bodies. To question what they were handed.
To remember that the voice of God does not only live in a pulpit or a printed page.
That's the shift. That's the reckoning.
That's the reintroduction to God through your own nervous system.
Your own knowing. Your own spirit.
We were never meant to make sense of the world based on what other people are saying.
We were meant to remember what we already know.

I didn't go into that conversation expecting a breakthrough.
I just knew I couldn't keep carrying beliefs I never gave myself permission to question.
And maybe that's where the true baptism begins.
Not in water, but in *remembrance*.
In peeling back every layer of performance until what's left is real, raw, and fully mine.
This wasn't about "winning" a conversation.
It was about reclaiming the right to have one.

To ask why I was taught what I was taught.

To name the confusion.

To trace the ritual back to its root.

To break the agreement with spiritual silence.

Because if the God I was told to believe in is real, then that God can handle my questions

And so, I'm not afraid anymore.

Not of a devil. Not of my doubt.

Not of what I might find when I ask the hard questions.

And my dad didn't have the answers.

But I got what I was looking for.

Because this wasn't just an interrogation for him.

It was a mirror for every woman reading this.

To look at the beliefs you've inherited.

The silence you've protected.

The rules you've obeyed without ever asking who wrote them.

This isn't rebellion.

This is return.

A return to *your* knowing.

A return to the voice that's always lived within you.

A return to the Divine that doesn't need to be decoded by preachers—

only remembered.

And they are going to be *shook* when they figure out

it was God that told me to write this book—

for you, and for me about seven years ago.

And it came through a prophet, a seer, in the church I grew up in.

It just took me silencing the noise—

to remember the sound of God in my own voice.

Where the Spell Breaks *(Interlude)*

It happened in my kitchen.
Over a bag of chips.
My daughter had just finished one and wanted more.
I told her no—
I wanted her to eat dinner.
She reached for my hand, trying to get me to grab the chips for
her.
I said, "No, baby. Don't do that."
And then she looked at me and said,
"Mommy, your bracelets are so pretty."
"I like your hair."
She smiled up at me so sweetly. So intentionally.
And in that moment, I felt the blood leave my face.

My spirit snapped.

Something hit me hard—
right in my chest.
Because I recognized what she was doing.
She was performing.
Trying to be sweet to earn a yes.
Trying to compliment her way into getting what she wanted.
Trying to earn something that should be freely given.

And it shattered me.

She's only three.
But the conditioning?
It's that deep.
This is how early we learn to shapeshift.
To please.
To over-function.

To perform our way into acceptance, into love, into approval.

So I got down on her level and said, "Listen to me.
Don't ever feel like you have to compliment me to get something.
Don't feel like you have to butter me up.
You don't have to earn my yes.
You don't have to perform for love."

That moment showed me just how quietly the trauma travels.
How early it sneaks in.
And how important it is that we catch it now.
She was born at a time when I was still under the spell.
Still unlearning.
Still breaking free.
But now?
Now I can see it in real time.
Now I can interrupt it with love.
Now the cycle ends.
Because healing doesn't just happen at the altar.
It doesn't just happen in books, workshops, or meditations.
It happens in kitchens.
Over bags of chips.
In the middle of everyday life.
Because Spirit can use anything.
God can use anything.

And that moment reminded me—
you don't have to be perfect to be powerful.
You just have to be present enough to see the pattern and choose
something different.
And that's exactly what I did.
That's what rebuilding belief looks like.
Not just in the big spiritual declarations.
Not just in what you call God.
Not just in how you define truth.

But in the small, sacred moments where you say:
"It stops with me."

Rebuilding belief means knowing you can interrupt the patterns.
That you can see the spell and not repeat it.
That you can raise your voice, or stay tender—
and still protect what's sacred.
That even if you were born into conditioning, you don't have to
pass it down.

Healing is part of the rebuild.
But this isn't just about healing.
This is about rewriting the rules.
This is about restoring the sacred.
This is about showing up—
different, rooted, awake.
And doing it again and again, one moment at a time.
Right there in your kitchen.
Right there in your spirit.
Right there in your bloodline.
That's rebuilding belief.

Chapter 10: Holy But Haunted

Some of y'all be looking good as hell on Sunday.
You show up to church in your skirt just below the knee—
like they trained you to.
Nice blouse. Edges laid. Light beat.
Some of y'all got on them little kitten heels that you only bring out
for first Sundays and funerals.
Bible in hand like a badge of honor.
After service, you post your little scripture on Facebook—
maybe a group picture with your girls in front of the altar like y'all
just left brunch instead of a sermon.
You don't miss a chance to say "God gets the glory."
You was loud as hell when you got baptized, too.
Posted the whole thing.
Captioned it "washed & redeemed."
But in private?
You're wrestling.
Not with demons.
With doctrine. With shame. With guilt.
With the gnawing question of why it still doesn't feel like peace—
even though you're doing everything "right."

And here's the part you don't say out loud:
You don't just wrestle with yourself.
You wrestle with other people's freedom.
You see a woman post something spiritual that doesn't include a
Bible verse, and you flinch.
You see somebody talk about their connection to God and they
don't mention church, and it irritates you.
You see a woman moving through the world in her truth, in her
joy, with her chest out and her spirit open, and it bothers you.
But let's pause right there:
Why?

Why does her freedom feel like a threat to your salvation?
Is it because your whole belief system was built on guilt?
Is it because were taught that shame was holy?
That being small made you worthy?
That modesty saved?
That obedience redeemed?
That pleasure was the gateway to hell?
So now when someone else decides they don't want to carry that weight—
you feel exposed.
Because you've been dragging chains behind you, calling it devotion.
And now you mad that somebody else laid theirs down and walked away smiling.

You want the truth?
You're not mad because it's "blasphemous."
You're mad because they ain't carrying the shame you're still stuck in.
That's what this is.
You're not offended. You're bitter.
Because you gave everything to the performance—
and they found peace in their truth.
Because you still cry over what they were bold enough to release.
You got baptized on Sunday and went back to that man on Monday.
You pray and still can't stop numbing.
You quote the Bible but you don't even like yourself.
You side-eye the woman who wears what she wants.
Who speaks how she wants.
Who worships how she wants—
or not at all.

Let me be real with you.
You don't want salvation. You want company.

You want to keep pretending while everybody else continues pretending with you.

You want to call it "righteousness," but it's just well-dressed repression.

Most of y'all aren't actually healing.

You're performing it.

And I know this may not be the read for the woman that has awakened, but I know there will be a woman that will accept my invitation, get this far into the journey, and still struggle to let go of her chains.

And nobody leaves my altar untouched.

Some of you think because you look the part, talk the part, post the part—

that you're whole.

But what you really are is stuck in one of the stages.

Let's break it down.

The 5 Stages of Spiritual Performance
(before embodiment ever touches down)

1. The Aesthetic Awakening

This is when someone first becomes interested in healing, self-love, or spirituality—but instead of doing the internal work, they go straight to the visuals:

- Sage bundles
- Crystals on the windowsill
- "Protect your peace" memes
- Outfits that look boho or "divine feminine"

It's not evil—it's a gateway.

But the problem is, they start to think *this* is the healing.

2. The Quote Prophet

They start reposting deep-sounding things:

- "Energy doesn't lie."
- "God removes people for a reason."
- "I'm not arguing, I'm protecting my peace."

They've mastered language without living it.
It's often a performance of boundaries they still don't actually hold.
It sounds strong, but it's usually coming from a place of unhealed resentment or ego-driven detachment.

3. The Timeline Therapist

Now they're speaking to others as if they've ascended.

- Giving advice to friends online
- Posting healing tips they don't apply
- Publicly calling out "low vibrational" people while still entertaining them in private

This stage is *wild* because it creates a false sense of superiority, but it's rooted in bypassing.
This is where a lot of people stall out because they start getting praise for the performance, and that praise *feels* like healing.

4. The Spiritual Performer in Crisis

At this point, life starts clocking them.

- The unhealed patterns resurface
- The relationship falls apart
- The trauma starts speaking louder than the quotes

And they start to feel disoriented.
Because the mask of healing stops working.

This is often when they'll either:
Double down and perform harder, or
Go silent, retreat, and actually start the real work.

5. The Quiet Becoming

This is the stage they never post about.

- No selfies, no sipping wine pics
- Just... silence, softness, self-confrontation
- Real boundaries, messy grief, inner child work

It's not aesthetic. It's not pretty.
But this is the moment embodiment finally begins.
And when you resurface?
You move different.
People feel it. And they don't know why.

So yeah.
Y'all are not doing altar calls.
You're doing shackle invitations.
You're standing at the front of the church saying,
"Here. Come get bound with me. I'm not free, but at least I look holy."

But let me offer you a different altar call.

One that don't require a white dress.
One that don't care if you got on lashes and lip liner.
One that don't start with shame and end in silence.

Say this prayer if you're ready to be released from the chains of indoctrination:

Spirit, I'm tired of pretending.
I release the shame that never saved me...

I release the performance that kept me small.
I choose truth, even when it makes people uncomfortable.
I choose freedom, even if it costs me approval.
I choose You, not the rules they told me I needed to reach You.
Let me be real. Let me be whole. Let me be free.

So be it.

Notice the shift that you felt when you prayed that prayer.
That wasn't coincidence.
That wasn't emotion.
That was your spirit responding.
And let's be honest—
How did you feel when you prayed that other prayer?
The one they told you to say at the front of the church.
The one they said would save you.
Did you feel anything?
Did you feel that lightness? Clarity? Truth?
Because I'll tell you right now—
I didn't.
I regurgitated that prayer years ago and felt… nothing.
I didn't understand it at the time.
But the day I chose myself, the day I finally said *"this ain't it"* and turned inward—
my whole body spoke.
And maybe… maybe yours did too.

And for those of you who didn't pray this prayer—
maybe because you don't feel like you're carrying guilt or shame.
Maybe because you don't think you're side-eyeing anybody.
Maybe you're just focused on your household.
Your peace. Your walk with God.

Let's talk about that.

Because your Bible says you're called to make disciples.
You're supposed to be saving souls, remember?
So why don't you care?
Why are you not out here evangelizing like it says?
Why are you picking and choosing which parts to obey?
If you have to question parts of it, why are you building your whole life around it?
If the only pieces you carry are the ones that make you look good, feel good, or post well, then what is it that you *actually* believe?
Because if you really believed *all* of it...
You'd still be stoning adulterers.
You'd still be silencing women.
You'd still be enslaving—
or being enslaved.

Don't talk to me about the Old and New Testament.
Because the truth is: y'all pick and choose because it doesn't make sense.
And you know it.
Y'all wear this religion like a badge of honor, but you're just now learning about the history.
You didn't know that this very doctrine was used to break you.
To erase you.
To justify your ancestors' captivity.
You praise a book that was once read to them with a whip in the other hand.
You defend it.
You build brands on it.
You post about it.

And then you look down on the women who say,
"I don't want to carry this anymore."

You call them rebellious.
But you won't even admit you're tired, too.

You keep showing up to the church with your mouth saying "yes"
while your body says "no."
You think the knots in your stomach are butterflies.
You think the lump in your throat is the Holy Spirit.
You think that constant pressure in your chest is conviction.
But baby, that's your nervous system trying to speak.
That fire in your belly?
That's not divine passion.
That's discernment.
That's your body begging you to wake up.
The last time I went to church, my spirit was screaming:
This ain't it.

And I finally listened.
Now I know the difference between reverence and repression.
Between God and guilt.
Between "conviction" and the ache of generational conditioning.
You're out here standing tall for a system that's been breaking
your back.
You've been praying to get free, but too scared to put the book
down.
You keep saying, "Any day now, it'll work."
But if God is infinite…
If God is powerful…
Then why hasn't it worked yet?
Maybe it's because you're not rebelling against God.
Maybe you're just finally rebelling against the chains they told you
were sacred.

Here's another altar call.
Say this if you're ready to come home to yourself:

Spirit, I see it now.
I've been worshipping the trauma in my bloodline.

Defending systems that never saw me as whole—only as something
to build on my back.
But I see clearly now...
The guilt doesn't belong to me.
The shame was never mine.
And I'm done calling bondage holy.

I choose truth, even when it disrupts everything.
I choose freedom, even when it's unfamiliar.
No more performance.
No more pretending.

Let me remember the wisdom in my bones.
Let me return to the source within me.
Let me know who I was before the chains.

So be it.

You've been called.
So answer—or stay haunted.

No reflection questions this time.
But I will leave you with space.
To name what came up—
not just in this chapter, but in the ones before it.
Maybe it's grief. Maybe it's rage.
Maybe it's something you can't name yet.
That's okay.
Let it settle.

Journal Space

Don't write what sounds good. Write what burns.

_____

_____

_____

_____

_____

_____

_____

_____

_____

_____

_____

_____

_____

_____

_____

_____

_____

_____

A Sip of Truth *(Interlude)*

Before we go any deeper, I need to slow down.
Not because I lost the flow —
but because I felt something come up in my spirit.
This wasn't part of the outline.
This wasn't planned.
But in the middle of writing this book I felt the need to pause.
Not to reflect on what came before.
Not to prepare for what's next.
But to speak directly to the part of you that's still quietly trying to
figure out what healing even means.
And what it's going to cost you.
As we continue to do a deep dive on our history, there may be
parts of you that unravel.
And I understand that you've done a lot of work to get to this point
and I want to honor that by saying first, I see you.

This isn't a historical lesson.
This isn't a theological breakdown.
This is a truth that showed up uninvited —
and would not let me move forward until I gave it voice.
So I'm giving it a name.
And a moment. And a page.

I know healing is the word on everybody's lips these days.
Everybody's got something to say about how to do it —
how hard it is.
But I wonder, how do they even know how hard healing really is,
If you've never truly surrendered to it?
I'm not saying people aren't trying.
I think most are doing the best they can —
with what they've been given.
And that was me once too.

Bleeding while believing.
Praying. Fasting. Giving.
Trying to earn my worth.
Trying to prove that I deserved to be whole.
That was the version of me who thought healing came through sacrifice.
The kind of sacrifice that left me empty.
But what I've learned is this—
real healing doesn't look like what most people are doing.
It's not a prayer without inner work.
It's not affirmations without aligned action.
It's not posting about healing while staying in the very environments that keep reopening the wounds.

You don't get to keep your comfort and evolve at the same time.
Healing *will* cost you.
It'll cost you your familiarity, your illusions, your coping mechanisms.
It might cost you relationships you once thought were permanent.
But in return, it gives you, *you*.
The version of you that remembers.
The version that doesn't shrink anymore.
When you come into my space, I'm not handing out prayers and band-aids.
I offer you a mirror, to face yourself.
And a scalpel—
to cut deep enough to free yourself.
And I know…
That's not what everybody's ready for.
Some of you made it through *The Awakened Woman*
And still chose to hide.
Still decided that your role—
Mother. Wife. CEO. Caregiver. Employee.
Was more worthy of protection than your soul.
Still decided to let other people think for you.

To let them decide what's too much.
What's acceptable.
What's wise.
That's why I didn't soften my tone here—
because I knew. I see you.

But let me ask you this:
Why did you get to the end of *The Awakened Woman* and still
decide that other people's comfort mattered more than your truth?
The only thing I was trying to persuade you to do is free yourself.
To do what's *truly* right for you—
without needing to think about somebody else first.
This isn't selfishness.
It's sacred reclamation.
Because no one is coming to save you.
And no one gets to live your life but you.
I know this shit is hard.
But I'm not telling you to do it because it's easy.
I'm telling you because it's *necessary*.
You're not going to grow clinging to what broke you.
You're going to grow the moment you decide you're done settling
for almost.
Almost healed.
Almost free.
Almost seen.
Almost loved.
No more almost.

So where do we go from here?

Get the fuck up.
Stop starving yourself.
Stop waiting for permission to choose you.
If I told you that your healing begins the moment you *decide*,
Would you still sit there and suffer?

It's like standing across the room from a cup of water—
thirsty as hell.
And instead of walking over and taking a sip, you keep saying
"But it's hard."
Yes, this shit is hard.
But it's also simple.
It starts with a *decision*.
Choose yourself.
Stop worrying about what church folks may think.
Stop worrying about that grown-ass man more than you worry
about your own peace.
Stop thinking your kids deserve your first sip.
They don't need your sacrifice.
They need your *overflow*.
And the only way they'll ever get that is if you start pouring into
you.
That's the real cheat code.

You think being the last to eat is love?
That giving until you're empty makes you holy?
It doesn't.
It makes you bitter.
And broken.
And the truth is—
while you keep clinging to the version of your life that's *killing*
you, your kids are watching.
Learning. Repeating.
They're learning how to survive instead of how to *live*.
How to suppress instead of feel.
How to neglect themselves just like you do.
You talk to yourself like shit.
And then wonder why your patience is gone.
You give everyone else the whole damn glass—
and can't figure out why there's nothing left for you.
I know this because I've lived it.

I've talked to women for hours.
Given them everything I had—
and still watched them walk away and choose the very pain that
broke them.
So I'm telling you now because I can.
Because I've been her.
Because I refused to keep bleeding for people who couldn't even
offer me a bandage.
So what now?
Are you going to keep babysitting grown-ass men?
Keep hiding behind your titles?
Your religion?
Keep calling sacrifice love and burnout purpose?
It's getting old, isn't it?
That's why you picked up this book in the first place.
Because something in you already knows.
So make a decision.
Right now.
This very second.
Choose you.

And when you walk to that metaphorical cup, when you finally
take that first sip—
don't be afraid of what's in it.
Don't overthink the flavor.
Just trust that it's exactly what your soul's been waiting for.
That's the art of surrender.
And that?
That's where your gospel begins.

Chapter 11: The Execution

And you know what?

Fuck the forbidden fruit.

Because now?

I am the tree.

Rooted. Reckoned with. Alive.

And every branch holds the wisdom they told us would kill us.

But they lied.

Knowledge never killed us.

Control did.

They taught us to fear questions.

To fear curiosity.

To fear ourselves.

But this chapter?

It's not about rebellion for rebellion's sake.

It's not about desecrating the sacred.

It's about demanding truth from the things we were told never to question.

It's about holding up a mirror to the systems that told us silence was holy and submission was salvation.

So let's ask what they prayed you'd never ask.

Why was divinity filtered through systems of oppression?

Why were sacred texts translated by kings, colonizers, and men with agendas?

Why does "the Word" get protected, but the people harmed by its misuse get ignored?

You want to talk about righteousness?

Let's talk about how Scripture was used to enslave, silence, and control.

You want to talk about reverence?

Let's talk about the blood on the pulpit and the shame in the pews.

Just like Jesus flipped tables in the temple, I'm flipping every misused verse and asking:
Was this really God or was this man?

If God values innocence, why did He command the slaughter of babies and nursing mothers during war? (1 Samuel 15:3)

If God is unchanging, why does He regret, repent, and reverse His own decisions in the Bible they call perfect? (Genesis 6:6, 1 Samuel 15:11, Jonah 3:10)

If the Bible is perfect, why does one verse say every soul is judged for itself — and another say God will curse bloodlines to the fourth generation? (Ezekiel 18:20, Exodus 34:7)

If God's Spirit lives inside me, why was I taught to silence the voice that lives in my own body? (John 16:13)

If the Gospel was supposed to set us free, why did they chain us with it instead? (Galatians 5:1)

If God's word is eternal, why did they insert the word "homosexual" in 1946 and change the meaning of love forever? (1 Corinthians 6:9 — original Greek vs 1946 RSV)

If God is sovereign, why would He entrust His holy word to slave owners, colonizers, kings, and councils? (Genesis 9:24–27, Council of Nicaea 325 AD, King James Version 1611)

If God values truth, why were lies about race, lineage, and worth embedded into sermons, policies, and laws? (Genesis 9:24–27)

If faith the size of a mustard seed can move mountains, why are generations still drowning under poverty, depression, and cycles of despair inside the church walls? (Matthew 17:20)

If salvation is a free gift, why does the church make you pay for it with your body, your loyalty, and your tithe envelope? (Galatians 2:16, 2 Corinthians 9:7)

If prayer moves mountains, why did our grandmothers die with Bibles under their pillows, begging for healing that never came? (James 5:15)

If the Kingdom of Heaven is already within me, why did they sell me a salvation I was born carrying? (Luke 17:21)

And my point is this—
if the Gospel was supposed to be good news, why has it been used like a noose around our necks for centuries?
I need you to sit with that. Really sit with it.
After years of studying and unlearning, I now understand why I had to write this gospel.
Someone had to break what's been binding us to a version of ourselves we were never meant to stay.

They call it rebellion. They call it dangerous.
They can call it whatever makes them feel safe.
I don't give a damn.
Because to me? This is reverence.
Not the quiet kind. Not the obedient kind.
But the kind that calls out what broke us.
The kind that tells the truth even when it shakes the room.
The kind that loves God *enough* to ask the hard questions.
This is reverence—
Stripped down.
Lit up.
And free.
This execution isn't the end. It's the beginning.

Chapter 12: Rebuilding Belief

You're not here to be told what to believe.
You're here to rebuild it.
To question. To expand.
To let what no longer fits… fall away.
You're allowed to change.
You're allowed to believe differently now.
And this time, let it feel like *freedom*.

I believe in God.
I believe there's a higher power orchestrating things I can't even explain.
But I also believe God is in me.
Not just beside me. *Within me.*
I believe I can trust my intuition and trust God.
That those two things aren't in conflict.
They're in collaboration.
I believe I can be spiritual and sexual.
Soft and sharp.
Still and seductive.
I can cry my eyes out one day and command a room the next.
I don't have to be one thing at a time.
I get to be everything.

There was a time when I thought my sensuality was shameful.
When I felt like loving sex made me less worthy of divine connection.
In fact, sex can feel like an act of worship to God—
with the right soul.
There was a time when I thought crying made me weak.
When being called "too emotional" felt like an insult.
Now?
I reclaim all of it.

My emotions are sacred.
My desires are divine.
My sensuality is a gift—
Not a sin.
You can feel me and still not figure me out.
That's the beauty of being a fully expressed woman.
You might meet me and not know what to call it.
But you'll know it's *real*.

Let's be honest—
They got one thing right in the church:
God is omnipotent. Omnipresent. Omniscient.
But what they didn't teach us is what that means *for us*.
That if we are made in God's image...
That means we carry power.
We are limitless.
We are sacred reflections of something eternal.
But when they gave God a face that didn't look like mine, a
colonizer's face—
They made it hard for me to see the God in *me*.
Now that I've removed that image, I can finally feel it:
I am aligned with divinity.
Not outside of it. *A part of it.*
This is what rebuilding belief looks like.
Not discarding God—
but discarding the version of God filtered through fear, control,
and colonization.
not rejecting your roots—
but refusing to be chained to someone else's definition of "holy."

You don't need to argue with anyone.
You don't need to defend your evolution.
But if someone tries to shrink your story down to something
you've outgrown?
You're allowed to speak up.

You don't have to be aggressive.
You don't have to be dismissive.
But you *can* be clear.
Because this right here?
This isn't just a belief system.
This is embodiment.
And when people say:
"Oh, it was God who brought you through…"

Yes, God carried you.
And the universe held you.
And Spirit guided you.
And you showed up.
You listened. You moved. You trusted.
This wasn't passive.
This was *active alignment*.
I went within.
I broke the cycles.
I did the work.
I'm not here because someone laid hands on me.
I'm here because *I* laid hands on my own heart—
And said, *we're not going back*.

Reflection Questions

1. What does freedom feel like in your bones? How does your body let you know you're no longer shackled?
2. What can you do now—emotionally, spiritually, physically—that you didn't feel free to do before?
3. When you breathe into your womb, your belly, your heart—what do you feel? What lives there now?
4. What belief are you ready to rebuild—not out of fear, but out of truth?

Journal Space

Don't write what sounds good. Write what burns.

_____

_____

_____

_____

_____

_____

_____

_____

_____

_____

_____

_____

_____

_____

_____

_____

_____

_____

Chapter 13: Colonized Attraction

It started with a scroll.

I wasn't searching for anything deep.

I was just trying to take a damn break.

I'd been editing for hours, and I told myself I needed to laugh, to nourish myself with something light before diving back in.

But that's when I came across the video.

It was a man talking about dating preferences—

specifically, how some white men claim they've never found a single Black woman attractive.

He said that's not just a "preference," it's racism.

And for some reason, that video stuck with me.

Something about that statement cracked something open.

I don't normally stop to examine why I like what I like.

I've always said I prefer Black men—

but I've never sat still long enough to ask why.

Or if that preference even belonged to me in the first place.

That video lit the match.

Because when you grow up in a certain kind of environment— low income, rough neighborhood, boys being rough around the edges—

you start to equate familiarity with safety. Even when it's not.

I didn't know I was doing it at the time, but looking back, it makes sense. The first boys I ever felt desire for looked like me, lived like me, moved like me. And even when they were mean to me, I still chased that dynamic.

I called it love. I called it chemistry.

I called it "he just has a lot going on."

I didn't call it what it was... conditioning.

I thought I was choosing my partners based on kindness or real attraction.

But if that were true, why the string of disrespectful, emotionally unavailable, aggressive-ass men?
If kindness were the criteria, why didn't I walk away when it wasn't present?
Because it wasn't about kindness.
It was about complexion.
It was about conditioning.
It was about colonization.

And I know that's a strong word. So let me be clear.

When I say colonization, I don't just mean a white man on a boat pulling up to the shores of your lineage.
I mean the slow stripping of your ability to choose for yourself.
I mean systems and social cues telling you who is safe, who is powerful, who is beautiful, who is worthy of desire.
I mean the way we start calling dysfunction "familiar," and pain "passion," and control "protection."
Colonization doesn't just invade your land.
It invades your preferences.
Your desire. Your discernment.
And this chapter isn't about telling you who to date.
It's about asking if you've ever questioned why.
Because when I dated a white boy, something felt different.
Not better. Not safer.
Just different.
And I had to ask myself:
Why did I feel that way?

Because when you grow up surrounded by struggle—
and the people around you are hurting, yelling, surviving—
whiteness starts to *feel* like the opposite of chaos.
But that's not truth.
That's programming.

And that means I have to be honest about what I've been taught to feel attracted to.
I realized I wasn't just craving love.
I was craving relief.
I was craving safety.
I was craving someone who wouldn't break me.
And sometimes that craving dressed up as preference.
As loyalty. As type.
But really?
It was a cry from my nervous system saying:
"Let me rest."

In this book and *The Awakened Woman*, we talked about the men.
We talked about patterns.
We talked about masculine wounds and our capacity to heal beyond them.
But we didn't stop long enough to ask:
Why do we keep choosing them?

Why do we feel that magnetic pull toward the ones who never earned our softness? Why does chaos feel like chemistry?
And how much of our "preference" is really just conditioning in disguise?
We say we want love.
But what we've really been trained to chase is familiarity.
And sometimes that familiarity feels like home —
even when it's built on harm.
So now I don't just ask:
Who do I find attractive?

I ask:
Does my body feel safe here?
Does my spirit feel seen?
Is this desire or is this duty?
Am I drawn or am I defaulting?

Because baby, attraction can be decolonized.
And when it is?
Desire gets to be honest.
It gets to be sacred. It gets to be soft.
And maybe for the first time in your life, you get to choose —
without the chain.

Reflection Questions

1. What did love and desire look like around you growing up? How did that shape what you chased?
2. Have you ever mistaken intensity for intimacy? What did that cost you?
3. When you feel "chemistry" with someone, where do you feel it in your body? Does it feel like safety or survival?
4. What does *true safety* in love feel like for your body, your spirit, your nervous system?

Journal Space

Don't write what sounds good. Write what burns.

_____

_____

_____

_____

_____

_____

_____

_____

_____

_____

_____

_____

_____

_____

_____

_____

_____

_____

_____

_____

_____

Chapter 14: The Investment

You were taught that 10% was the seed.
But what if the real breakthrough came when you started pouring
that same 10% back into *you*?
Not into a basket.
Not into a pastor's vacation fund.
Not into a building project.
But into your healing. Your growth. Your *freedom*.
They've got people believing that the currency of heaven is *money*
when really—
it's devotion to self.
To knowing yourself. To owning yourself.
To discerning the lies from the truth.
To rebuilding belief in your own divine instruction.

The real product of the church is not transformation.
It's the next feel-good message.
They pass it out every Sunday and maybe again on Wednesday if
you're really devoted.
A little hope. A little guilt.
And if you're lucky?
You might walk out of there feeling worthy—
for a few hours.
But they don't teach you how to build.
They don't teach you how to discern.
They don't teach you how to own your yes or your no.
They teach you how to give.

But imagine if instead of dropping that 10% into a basket every
week, you dropped it into:
- A savings account
- A Roth IRA
- A therapist's office

- A coach who holds you accountable
- A writing workshop
- A business course
- A vision board
- A deep rest day
- A massage
- A passport renewal
- A healing retreat

You know what you have after that?
A *foundation*.

This chapter isn't about whether God is real.
We already know Spirit is real.
This is about what they taught you.
They taught you that the only way to receive financial abundance was through that 10%.
And that's not true.
For those of you that I taught you how to reclaim your limitless self, what shifted?
Did things begin to flow to you with more ease?
Did you feel more grounded, more confident, freer?
And if not—
What changed? What didn't?
Because if you're still tying your worth and your wealth to that 10%...
Maybe it's time to start investing in the one thing you've never been taught to trust:
You.

They told you the tithe was a sacrifice.
But they never told you that self-betrayal was the real cost.

That every time you dropped that 10% in the basket, while ignoring the calling on your own life, you weren't making a spiritual deposit—
You were going into spiritual debt.
Because the church doesn't ask you to build yourself.
They ask you to believe in something *outside* of yourself.
They'll tell you to pray for provision, while they collect a check.
They'll say God will multiply what you give, but they don't teach you how to multiply anything on your own.
That's not faith. That's codependency.
That's religious capitalism wrapped in scripture.
It's a divine guilt trip.
They sell you on the idea that if your breakthrough hasn't come, it's because you weren't faithful enough.
Not because you weren't resourced, supported, or informed.
But because you didn't believe enough.
You didn't give enough. You didn't attend enough. You didn't submit enough.
But what if submission isn't spiritual at all—
Unless it's aligned?
What if it becomes self-abandonment when it's demanded by institutions that want your devotion—
but fear your discernment?

So let me ask you this:
What if you redirected that 10%?
Not just the money—
but the energy.
The spiritual labor. The guilt. The time.
Imagine if all of that was poured into healing your nervous system, mastering your gifts, anchoring your voice, building something that outlives you.
Imagine if *you* were the offering.
Because that's the real revolution.

Not taking your hands off the wheel and hoping God shows up.
But realizing *you* are the vessel.
You are the miracle.
You are the foundation you've been waiting on.

Before you turn the page, breathe.
Think about what you've been giving.
Your energy. Your devotion. Your time.
Now ask yourself:
Is that investment rooted in fear? Or in freedom?

Let your next yes be holy.
Let your next no be sacred.
And may every offering you give from now on... include you.

Chapter 15: Adornment Is Activism

I didn't wake up one day and say, "Let me become that woman."
I just started listening to my body.
And without realizing it, the soft pinks stopped calling me.
The gold started whispering.
The scents became sacred.
What began as instinct became ritual.
I stopped reaching for the things that used to feel like "me."
I started gravitating toward bold patterns, earthy tones—
fabrics that flowed and draped and felt like home.
It was like my spirit had outgrown who I used to be.
And now she wanted to be seen—
not just through my body, but through my frequency.
When I started layering my perfume with intention—
same order, same areas of the body each time—
I didn't realize I was conjuring memory.
But that's exactly what it became:
A scent of remembrance.
A coded frequency.
A spell.

Women and men alike started saying the same thing:
"You smell... addictive."

And I smiled.
Because they were right.
It wasn't just the perfume.
It was my energy. My presence. My remembrance.
And it was radiating out of every pore.
See, there's a reason people start looking at you differently when
you reclaim your roots.
It's not because you're trying to be seen.
It's because you're channeling something ancient.

You're becoming a mirror of what's been lost—
and people *feel that*.
There's a reason people stare when I wear my headwrap.
Or when I'm laced in beads and walking with my shoulders back.
They're not just looking at me.
They're witnessing memory made visible.
Because this isn't just clothing.
This is ancestral technology—
coded memory, layered meaning, protective signal.

Let's talk about history for a moment because this isn't new.
This is old power resurfacing.
In many African societies, adornment wasn't performance—
it was *language*.
Beads told stories. Colors marked rites of passage.
Jewelry protected the spirit and signaled power.
Headwraps weren't just about modesty, they were crowns.
Nails, gold, body paint—
All of it meant something.
The body wasn't just dressed.
It was *coded*. Activated. Honored.
And when colonizers came, they feared that power.
They called it vanity. They stripped it down.
They replaced sacred expression with forced assimilation.
And we've been shrinking in our own clothes ever since.

But not anymore.

Now, I don't dress for attention.
I dress for alignment.
When I wrap my head, I'm protecting my crown.
When I layer my perfume, I'm layering intention.
When I put on gold, I'm calling my ancestors forward.
When I choose my outfit, I ask:
"What am I activating today?"

Because every single piece carries frequency.
And every time I get dressed, I'm choosing which one to walk in.
There's a difference between being seen and being witnessed.
And when you start dressing from the inside out, you'll notice the shift.
People no longer lust after you.
They *revere* you.
They *honor* you—
even if they don't understand why.
It's not because you've become intimidating.
It's because you've become unreachable by those not on your frequency.
You are no longer dressing to seduce.
You're dressing to declare.

But let's go a little deeper about why I cover my head.
Covering the head during prayer is not just about reverence.
It's about protection.
Think about the different Chakras or energy centers.
Crown chakra? That's your divine connection.
Third eye? That's your inner vision and discernment.
And when you're channeling, praying, sensing, receiving—
those centers are wide open.
And since I have tapped into my seer gift, I'm constantly *seeing* and channeling—
so I'm wide open.
And I cover my head for the same reason I protect my womb:
Because my body is a sacred gateway.
And I don't leave sacred gateways exposed.
You don't cover your head to "get to God."
You cover it because you are with God—
and you're keeping everything else the fuck out.

I mentioned earlier in the book that people in the church plays
would wear white shawls on their head without ever questioning
what is actually does for them.
That's what I'm talking about.
People wear the thing. They don't carry the thing.
They've been performing protection without actually protecting a
damn thing. Because they don't even know what's under the cloth.
They don't even know how open they really are.

But I do.

Because I've felt the pressure in my head when I didn't wear it.
Because I've walked into rooms and left with energy that wasn't
mine. Because the moment I started wearing it intentionally—
everything shifted.
The headaches stopped. The noise quieted. The channel cleared.
This isn't about religion. This is about energetic awareness.
This is about not walking through spiritual war zones with your
gates wide open.

So no—
I don't wrap my head because I'm trying to look holy.
I wrap it because I am holy.
And no one needs to understand it.
Because this isn't for them. This is for me. And for you.
For the you who forgot how sacred she is.
For the you who was told to tone it down.
For the you who now remembers:
You were never meant to be soft-spoken in your frequency.
You're not "doing too much."
You're doing what your lineage requires.

The Dressing Room

Let's be real.
Are you dressing for alignment or acceptance?
Be honest.
Do you really love those short French tips?
Or is it because someone told you they're "classy"?
Are you into dainty tattoos or did someone just teach you that
boldness is too much?
Are you slicking your hair back tight because it feels like you?
Or because it's what's most digestible?

This didn't start with society. This started in sanctuaries.
We were told red was sinful.
That long nails meant lust.
That gold was for vanity.
That a woman who stood out was seeking attention—
and not the holy kind.
We were taught to dress like we were *avoiding hell*, not
embodying heaven.
So it's no wonder some of us still feel guilt when we want to
shine. No wonder some of us still shrink when we feel too
magnetic.

But let me one to tell you:
Your nails are wands.
Your hair is a statement.
Your scent is memory.
Your clothing is frequency.
Adornment has always been sacred. We just forgot.
There's nothing wrong with simplicity.
There's nothing wrong with soft.
But let's tell the truth—
Are you being true to *you*, or are you still performing?

So ask yourself:

- Where did you learn your definition of "classy"?
- Who told you boldness was "too much"?
- What part of you are you still dimming to be more palatable?

You don't have to go out and change your whole aesthetic.
But I want you to check your why.
Because sacred adornment is not about impressing.
It's about expressing. It's about remembering.
So when you look in the mirror tomorrow, ask yourself:
"Is this really me?
Or is this who I thought I had to be to be accepted?"

Because you were never meant to be muted.
You were meant to move like a memory.
To walk like a portal. To adorn like a priestess.

Chapter 16: She Who Carries the Flame

What is the flame?

It's not hustle. It's not hardness. It's not a performance.

It's the fire in your chest that tells you the truth—

without needing proof.

It's your discernment.

Your calling. Your boundaries.

Your energy. Your presence.

The flame is what got reignited in you the moment you

remembered who you were.

But remembering wasn't the hardest part.

Carrying it is.

Carrying the flame means choosing peace over proving.

It means you don't respond to everything that tries to pull you out

of alignment. You don't match people's chaos just to show them

you're not the one. You already know you're not the one.

You don't have to say it.

You just *are* it.

Because the woman who carries the flame doesn't argue.

She doesn't defend.

She doesn't entertain passive-aggressiveness or projections.

She sees it. She feels it. She names it—

internally, and keeps it moving.

She doesn't have to announce that she's powerful.

People feel it when she walks in the room.

That's what energy protection is.

Not just saying no to a request.

But saying no to the energy underneath it.

Blocking.

Walking away.

Not responding.

Not staying where it doesn't feel safe.

Not going where her spirit says no.
Not attaching just because there's a history.

The woman who carries the flame is deeply intentional.

She's not cold. She's clear.
She's not aggressive. She's anchored.
She doesn't speak unless it's true, necessary, and aligned.
She has nothing to prove—
because her energy speaks first.
She doesn't say "yes" to be liked.
She doesn't post every win to be seen.
She doesn't over-explain to be understood.
She protects her energy like it's sacred.
Because it *is*.

Let me tell you what carrying the flame looks like in real life:
It's not one single moment.
It's a thousand micro-decisions.
It's silence in a meeting when someone's being passive-
aggressive, and you know it's not yours to carry.
It's reading an email laced with coded language, clocking the
energy, and refusing to give it breath.
It's sensing a shift in someone's tone—
how they soften, how they stutter, how they fumble when their
aggression meets your groundedness.
You don't respond with pettiness. You don't raise your voice.
You *hold your frequency*.
Because you've mastered your emotions.
And once you've done that?
You realize how fruitless it is to meet people in their storm.
And when it comes to your personal life?
Carrying the flame looks like saying:
"I don't like the way you handled that."
"This is what I need moving forward."

And then walking away if it's not honored.

Maybe you say it once.
Maybe not at all.
Maybe you block.
Maybe you leave.
Maybe you just go silent and stop showing up.
Not because you're afraid.
But because you finally understand that people are showing you who they are.
They're not confused. And neither are you.
Energy protection is radical.
And it's not just about other people.
It's about *you*.
It's about not oversharing just to feel close to someone.
It's about not performing transparency when silence would feel safer.
It's about not documenting your healing journey in real time.
Not because you're hiding, but because some things are sacred.
People didn't know I was birthing a book until I was done writing that motherfucker.
Not because I feared sabotage—
but because Spirit already said *yes*.
I didn't need to say it out loud.
I needed to *protect* it.
And that's the difference.

You're not here to be seen anymore.
You're here to be sovereign.
You're not here to be impressive.
You're here to be in integrity.
You don't owe anybody access.
You don't owe anybody updates.
You don't owe anybody a damn thing except the truest version of yourself.

That's why you no longer carry people who don't want to walk beside you.

That's why you don't chase clarity from people who benefit from your confusion.

And that's why, if you're still out here overgiving, overexplaining, overextending—
you're not carrying the flame.

You're fanning someone else's.

You know better now.

And the woman who carries the flame?

She protects herself like a temple.

She holds silence like a weapon.

She sets boundaries without guilt.

She chooses herself without apology.

And she knows this:

If it doesn't feel right in her spirit, she doesn't go.

If it doesn't sound right in her bones, she doesn't explain.

If it doesn't align with her peace, she doesn't engage.

She is fire.

And fire doesn't chase.

It *burns steady*.

You've done the remembering.

Now this is about protecting what you remembered.

This is about moving like a woman who's been anointed.

Not with oil.

But with clarity.

So walk like it.

Speak like it.

Say no like it.

Release like it.

You carry the flame now.

Act accordingly.

Protecting the Flame

You've felt the flame.
Now ask yourself—
Am I really carrying it?
Or am I still dimming it just to make people comfortable?

Let's go deeper:
- Where are you still matching energy you've already outgrown?
- Where are you explaining your clarity to people who've already shown they don't respect it?
- Where are you shrinking to avoid being "too much" again?

Also want to know...
Where have you been gaslighting yourself?
Telling yourself it's not that bad.
Telling yourself maybe *you* just need to try harder.
Telling yourself this is just a lesson—
when your spirit's been whispering *get out*.
Because the woman who carries the flame?
She doesn't call red flags "growth."
She calls it what it is—
misalignment.
She doesn't babysit dysfunction and call it love.
She doesn't perform peace when her body is screaming.
She knows her boundaries don't need justification.
Her discernment isn't up for debate.
Her energy is sacred and not everyone gets access.

So ask yourself:
- What would it look like to protect your flame for real?
- What would it feel like to walk away without overexplaining?

- What are you still calling peace when it's really performance?

Because this isn't about being liked.
This is about being *lit*—
with clarity, with conviction, with wholeness.
And you don't need permission to burn.
You just need to remember who the flame belongs to.

I've given you enough to think about, now reflect.

Journal Space

Don't write what sounds good. Write what burns.

_____

_____

_____

_____

_____

_____

_____

_____

_____

_____

_____

_____

_____

_____

_____

_____

_____

_____

_____

_____

Chapter 17: Your Body Is the Church

I used to think spirituality only counted if it looked like a
ceremony.
If it sounded like a hymn. If it happened behind church doors.
But now I know better.
Now I know that the pulpit isn't in a building. It's in me.
And my body?
That's the church.
Let me tell you what happened to me one day.
I pulled into the Dunkin' drive-thru to get a *hot vanilla chai latte*.
That was supposed to be a quick, nothing moment.
When the young woman came on the speaker, she couldn't hear
me clearly. I had to repeat myself a few times.
And I heard it in her voice—
tight, tense, like she was already bracing for someone to snap.
She said, "I'm not trying to be rude, but I can't hear you."
I knew that voice. I've had that voice.
The one that's trying to take up as little space as possible just to
make it through the day.
The one that's been trained to apologize for existing.
So when I got to the window, I asked, "Who took my order?"
And when she stepped up, I looked her dead in her eyes and asked,
"Who told you it was rude to ask someone to speak up?"
She laughed, but I knew that laugh.
That laugh meant: *Damn. She saw me.*
She told me how people get upset with her all the time, just for
asking to hear them better.
And I said, "You're not rude. You're doing your job. Stop
apologizing. They're just projecting."
She smiled and thanked me like her whole spirit had just exhaled.
And then they handed me my chai... and I drove away.
I was about two minutes away from my office when I took my first
sip and realized it was made wrong.

I looked at my cup and smiled.

Because I'm awake now.

And when you're awake, even a messed-up coffee means something.

And knowing that—

I turned my car around and went back.

As I waited inside for them to remake it, I stood there staring at the doughnuts.

You know how you try to act like you're not going to get one?

But the longer you stare, the more you know it's over for you?

Yeah. That was me.

I looked at the woman behind the counter and said,

"You had me standing here long enough to want a doughnut. Now I must have one."

We both laughed.

And then the woman I affirmed earlier walked over and told her not to charge me.

And immediately I thought to myself...

She didn't do that because I was nice.

She did that because I reminded her—

who the fuck she was.

That's what this is. That's what this walk is about.

Being so embodied in your truth that your presence activates people.

That's church. That's *the gospel*.

That's what they don't teach you in colonized religion.

That the altar isn't in some faraway place. It's in your body.

That the sermon isn't only in scripture—

it's in your energy.

And sometimes, the assignment isn't a deep revelation.

Sometimes the assignment is just to remind another woman not to shrink.

Before I walked out, I looked at her again and said,

"Remember what I said. Don't apologize to nobody."

Then I sat in my car. Took a sip of my remade chai.
And that shit still wasn't right.
I laughed.
Threw my car in drive.
And drove to a Circle K to get some damn cream.
The thing is… the drink was never the point.
The order didn't matter.
The drive-thru was the altar.
My voice was the sermon.
And the woman behind the window?
She was the reason I was sent.
They don't tell you that awakening won't always feel magical.
That it won't always look holy
Sometimes it looks like errands and cravings, and a coffee that
doesn't taste right.
But your presence shifts shit. Your energy carries the flame.
That's what I meant in *The Awakened Woman* when I said:
"I am the temple. I am the altar. I am the offering. I am the fire."

That wasn't poetry. That was truth.
And this?
This was the real-life version.
I didn't need a pulpit.
I didn't need to lay hands.
I didn't need tongues or scripture. Just remembrance.
And to hold space for someone else to remember too.
This is what it means to embody your spirituality.
To stop outsourcing your power.
To stop waiting for a sacred moment—
and become the sacred moment.
You don't need to chase the divine.
The divine is already in you.
You are the sermon.
You are the church.

And yes… even with nasty ass coffee—
You are still the miracle.

The Inner Invocation

I want you to think about this:
What if your power isn't just in how you show up when everything is aligned—
What if it's also in how you respond when everything goes left?

Think about the last time something didn't go your way:
A wrong order.
A delay.
A detour.
A moment that felt off or inconvenient.

Now ask yourself:
- Was that an inconvenience or an invitation?
- Was that a mistake or a message?
- Did that detour pull you off track or was it the track?

What if it was all sacred?
What if the universe was using that moment to slow you down, to wake you up, to place you in position?
Because this is what sacred leadership really is:
It's presence.
It's responsiveness.
It's remembering that the Divine is never late, never early—
always aligned.
It's understanding that your life is the altar.
And you are always in ceremony.

Reflection Questions

1. In what small ways has the universe been calling you to lead?
2. When's the last time someone softened in your presence, and you didn't even realize you were the reason?
3. Where have you been the offering, the altar, the fire—and overlooked the sacredness of your own power?
4. Do you know what it feels like to walk through the world and know that you are the church?

Journal Space
Don't write was sounds good. Write what burns

Chapter 18: The Suture

I don't know if it was after the first book, before, or somewhere in between—

but there was a point where I asked myself if it was possible to go back to my old life.

Not because I wanted to—

but because I was afraid I *could*.

And that fear didn't come from a lack of self-trust.

It came from the weight of how far I'd come.

From the knowing that I've healed so much, I've remembered so much, that the real test would always be what happened when the old life tried to come back.

Because I remember what it felt like when he called.

My child's father.

Gone for months, sometimes a year.

No presence. No consistency.

And then, out of nowhere, he'd call.

All the apologies. All the promises.

And I'd get pulled right back in.

I used to eat that shit up.

So even though I felt whole now, even though I had mastered my "no," I still questioned...

Could I get pulled back?

Because it's easy to set boundaries in still waters.

The real test is when the tide returns—

when the thing that once broke you to your core knocks on your door again—

then we'll see.

Let me tell you something.

When I got that letter in the mail telling me I had to go to court, and had to see that man again after nine months of silence?

I felt the blood drain from my face.

Not because I was afraid of *him*.
But because I knew what I was really facing...
Her.
The old version of me.
The woman who didn't know how to say no.
The woman who mistook struggle for love.
The woman who let promises override patterns.
The woman who was still learning her power.
That court date wasn't about him.
It was about *her*.
It was about honoring who I've become in front of the very energy
I had to fight my way out of.
It was about proving to myself that I didn't just survive that
version of me—
I transcended her.

That was the suture.

That moment stitched closed what had been leaking for far too
long.
That ache?
That longing?
That "maybe someday" I never wanted to admit I still carried?
It got cauterized the moment I realized I didn't shake when I heard
his voice.
It got sealed the moment I spoke clearly in front of a judge and
asked:
"What's the next step if I don't want to pursue child support?"

Because what I was really saying was:
I don't need anything else from him.
Not money.
Not answers.
Not presence.
Not potential.

Not closure.
Not even child support.
That part of me—
closed herself.

This is what The Suture means.

She who remembers does not leak.
She who remembers does not hemorrhage where she once ached.
She who remembers doesn't keep reopening old wounds just to see
if they still hurt.
She who remembers seals herself.
She wraps herself in grace.
She releases the urge to explain, to wonder, to wait.
She who remembers no longer builds altars around abandonment.
She no longer hopes the absent will return.
She no longer craves from the hands that once emptied her.
She who remembers doesn't just survive.
She sutures.

So no, May 7th didn't mean shit to me.
It was just the appointment that confirmed what I already knew in
my spirit:
I'm healed.
I'm whole.
I'm home.
I've done the work.
I've met the ache.
I've sealed the leak.
And I have nothing left to prove to the person who stopped
showing up.
You are not my scar anymore.
You are my seal.
And I release you.
For real this time.

And after the court hearing, I had a vision.
I saw myself laying on a cold metal table.
Not afraid. Not resisting. Just ready.
I felt everything.
The temperature in the room. The pressure.
A thick needle pressed into my skin, puncturing deeply—
and I welcomed it.
Because I knew this wasn't harm.
It was the final thread pulling through.

Then the vision flashed.

I was upright in a hospital bed.
Contractions seconds apart.
I was calm. Still.
Breathing through each wave because I knew something divine
had its hands on me.

Back to the table.

The thread moved again—
Tightening. Securing. Sealing.

And then another flash:
My baby was crowning.
I was still breathing. Still calm. Still open.
And then—
an explosion.
A golden light erupted.
I couldn't name what was born.
I only knew...
it was here.
Something I had carried for lifetimes.
Something I had been prepared to deliver through fire.

And in that moment, I knew—
the bleeding had stopped.
The seal was final.
And maybe that's what this chapter is for you too—
not just a memory…
but the moment you stopped leaking.
For me, it was a letter in the mail.
A court date.
A man who used to represent everything I had to fight to escape.
But for you?
It might not be a man.
Maybe it's the addiction.
Maybe it's the needle, the bottle, the bag, the high you swore
you'd never chase again.
Maybe it's the religious trauma—
the guilt that still whispers when you try to trust your own voice.
Maybe it's family—
the ones who break you with a smile.
Who say "we love you" but only when you're convenient.
Maybe it's not fear of losing progress.
Maybe it's fear that the old you could still rise and undo it all.
The you who didn't think she could survive without the chaos.
The you who used to call pain "normal."
The you who kept bleeding just to prove she could still stand.

So if that's you—
let me tell you something:
You can do this.
Close your eyes.
Picture yourself on the table.
Breathe.
Imagine the needle puncturing your skin.
And don't flinch.
This is the stitch that seals the leak.
This is the moment the bleeding stops.

Let the thread pull through.
Let the pain pass.
Let the wound close.
You are being sutured.
Say this to yourself, out loud if you can:

I am ready to be closed.
I am ready to stop leaking where I once bled.
I am not afraid of the needle, the thread, or the healing.
I will not flinch when the old life tries to return.
I will not bow to the cravings, the chaos, or the lies.
I am sealing what once broke me.
I am whole.
I am here.
I am held.
And this time, I am not reopening.
Not for guilt.
Not for nostalgia.
Not even for love.

And breathe.

Chapter 19: The Last Supper

I write this chapter from a place of grief.

A place of remembrance.

A place where sacred clarity found me—

in the middle of a clearance aisle.

I thought I was just going into Burlington to get my daughter some shoes. But when your body becomes a living altar, Spirit will meet you anywhere.

I wasn't praying. I wasn't meditating.

I wasn't at the front of a church.

I was between errands—

walking through rows of discounted décor, minding my business, when I saw it: a picture of The Last Supper.

I snapped a photo.

No big moment. No spiritual theatrics.

Just… click. And kept walking.

It wasn't until I sat down later that the weight of it dropped in.

I stared at that image, one I've seen since I was a little girl—

and suddenly, I felt something crack open.

Grief.

Confusion.

Rage.

And something else I couldn't name yet.

Because while most people see that image and think of holiness, sacrifice, and salvation—

I saw distortion.

I saw performance.

I saw power stripped and repackaged.

I saw a prophet whose truth was turned into a trap.

Because I'm a seer.

I see through things.

And when I looked at that painting… I didn't just see Jesus.

I saw myself.
A woman blazing the same trail they propped him up for.
A guide.
A revealer.
A mirror.
A mouthpiece for Spirit.

People don't like when I say that.
Because if he's not the only one—
then they'd have to remember who they are, too.
But if he came to remind us of who we are, then why are we still
bowing instead of becoming?
That's what they never told you:
Communion was never supposed to be a ritual.
It was supposed to be a remembrance.
But instead of remembering the God in themselves, they
romanticized the God in him.
They sip the juice and eat the wafer as if that makes you whole,
while ignoring the very thing he came to teach you—
that you are divine too.
They love to worship his sacrifice, but they've never honored their
own.

Before this moment...
I imagine that you've never asked what your soul had to endure
just to survive this life.
You've never broken your own bread.
You've never poured your own wisdom.
Because that's what the bread and the blood really were.
The bread was his breaking.
The blood was his becoming.
And when I talk about bleeding on the pages, when I say I've
cracked wide open, I'm not being poetic—
I'm living what he modeled.
This isn't just a metaphor.

This is *the gospel*.
The real one.
The one your bones already knew before the world tried to make you forget.

So come.
Let's take communion.
Not to be forgiven—
but to remember what's always been yours.
Break the bread—
For the women who fed others while starving themselves.
For the parts of you that had to die just so this one could live.
Sip the wine—
not to erase your past, but to honor it.
To pour libation for every ancestor who prayed you'd rise.

I wrote this chapter to remind you that your wounds are sacred—
not just his.
Because somewhere along the way, we were taught to worship his breaking while denying our own.
We were taught to romanticize his sacrifice while silencing the places we still bleed, but communion was never meant to make you small. It was meant to remind you that your body is sacred, too.
Your breaking.
Your pouring.
Your resurrection.
It all matters.
You weren't put here just to bow at someone else's altar.
You were called to build your own.
That your becoming is divine.
This chapter is your permission slip.
So when you break the bread and sip the wine—
don't just remember *him*.
Remember you.

A Final Word

We named the colonizers.
We exposed the lies.
We remembered the conjure women.
The seers.
The midwives.
The medicine women.
We talked about blood, birth, power, presence, and the altar in your chest.
But maybe what we really did here...
Was remind you that you're not broken.

You've been burned out because you've been trying to carry sacred fire inside systems that were built to smother you.
That's not your fault, but it *is* your responsibility now.
Because once you know what you carry—
you can't keep acting like you don't.
Maybe you've been waking up tired not because you need more sleep, but because you're tired of pretending your job is the assignment.
Maybe the deep sigh you let out every Sunday night isn't just about Monday.
It's your soul whispering: *this can't be it*.
And no—
I'm not telling you to quit your job today. But I am telling you to stop lying to yourself about why you're so tired.
Because when the work is aligned with your gift, it might stretch you, but it doesn't drain you like this.

So ask yourself:
- Are you exhausted or are you suppressing your gifts?
- Are you burnt out or are you meant to lead differently?

- Are you showing up or are you shrinking to survive?

You weren't called to burn out. You were called to burn brighter.
That's what this whole book was about.
Not just remembering, but never forgetting again.
You've already awakened.
Now it's about keeping the flame lit.
Even when your environment tries to make you small.
Even when your calendar fills with things that aren't aligned.
Even when you're the only one who sees what's sacred.

You are the flame.
You are the altar.
You are the medicine.
You are the one who knows.

I had been bleeding and breaking for years before I was ready to answer the call.
But when the time came—
I had no regrets.
Even now, as I write this with tears in my eyes, I wouldn't change a thing because I needed those moments.
Those aches. Those spirals. Those initiations.
I needed them so I could transmute them.
So I could write the guide.
So I could tend the flame that was sparked in you the moment you picked up *The Awakened Woman*.
And maybe God could have used someone else.
Another woman. Another vessel. Another name.
But I'm the one who said yes.
The one who cracked when it mattered.
So why not me?
That's the question I ask every time I'm tempted to complain.
Every time it gets inconvenient, hard, or heavy.

If I have the ability to alchemize the way that I do—
then I'm the one.
I'm the one who remembered.
I'm the one who surrendered.
I'm the one who said yes.
I'm the one who cracked open and let God come through.
Twice. In one year.
I didn't expect to birth two books this year.
But this is what happens when you recognize the God in you—
You become limitless.
And I am.

And you are too.

I told you earlier in the book how a prophet visited a church I used
to attend.
She looked me in the eyes and said I would write a book.
She didn't know me.
She didn't know what I carried.
She had no idea she was prophesying a gospel.
One that would dismantle everything they told us to believe.
But she knew enough to speak it, and I knew enough to write it.
And my father recorded that moment and kept it after all these
years. When I published my first book, he made it his mission to
find it and send it to me. I cried watching it because I thought she
was out of her mind when she told me I was an Oracle, and that I
would produce several books. She knew I'd be walking women
through their healing.

This is why I no longer overplan.
I'm not trying to predict what's next.
I'm just going where Spirit tells me to go.
Because now—
I'm doing what I never imagined because I surrendered to the call.
Maybe you're feeling a pull now, too.

Maybe someone told you years ago that you would do something
you never imagined.
You feel it.
That knowing?
That's your next chapter.
Or maybe…
It's the book you were meant to write.
And if it is—
welcome home.

House of Her Publishing is waiting for you.

A Blessing for the Road Ahead

May you walk like you know who you are—
even when the world forgets.
May you trust your "no" without guilt—
and your "yes" without apology.
May your softness never be mistaken for weakness—
and your strength never confused for hardness.
May you never again shrink to be digestible.
May you never again silence your body to soothe someone else's
discomfort.

May your rituals be yours.
May your voice be yours.
May your life be yours.

And when the old cycles come knocking—
may you meet them not with fear, but with fire.
Because you've already broken them.
You don't owe anyone proof of your power.
You only need to stay rooted in it.
This path didn't start here and it sure as hell doesn't end here.
So if you're ready—
hand on your heart, hand on your womb, and breathe deeply.

Be still for a moment.

And when you're ready... snap your fingers.
Not because this is a performance—
but because this is a remembering.
And that snap?
That's your initiation.
And when you rise tomorrow, may your first breath be a vow to
never betray yourself again.